MILLENNIALS

MILLENNIALS

DELANO PERRY

BMcTALKS Press
4980 South Alma School Road
Suite 2-493
Chandler, Arizona 85248

Volume pricing is available to bulk orders placed by corporations, associations, and others. For details, please contact BMcTALKS Press at info@bmtpress.com

FIRST EDITION

Library of Congress Control Number: 2020909327

ISBN: 978-0-9998901-7-2

TABLE OF CONTENTS

DEDICATION

This book is dedicated to all the millennials out there. Even though we are often on the receiving end of stereotypes and name calling. Millennials are a unique generation. They have survived everything life has thrown their way. They survived the Great Recession of 2008 and the rising costs of living and education. It is about time for millennials to be understood and respected instead of receiving a stigma. I would also like to dedicate this book to my cousin, Brittney Perry. May you continue to rest in peace.

CHAPTER 1

You Just Don't Understand

MILLENNIALS

Millennials, in my humble opinion, must be the most judged and misunderstood generation alive! We—and I write "we" because I am a millennial—rarely catch a break. We are labeled lazy, entitled, narcissistic, and job-hoppers. Well, I am here to burst a few bubbles, but we will get to that in a few. My question to Generation X and baby boomers is what did the generations before you think about you? Every generation tends to look at the generation that follows as if they don't fit the mold. Guess what. Who cares?

We are unique individuals, and no one said we have to be the way you want us to be. William Strauss and Neil Howe are often credited with naming Generation Y millennials, but we have also been called "echo boomers" because of increasing birth rates between the 1980s and 1990s. Some tend to compare us to the Greatest Generation. How do you feel about that, Gen X and boomers? Okay, okay. I digress, but in the words of Bryan "Birdman" Williams, "put some respek on our name." I am willing to bet most of you "old heads" do not know who that is, but hey, you all have said way worse things about us millennials.

Yes, I will use some improper grammar, and yes, I may reference people and quotes that only a millennial may understand. But guess what. That's just my sense of entitlement kicking in. So, if you are out of the loop or are not hip, then this may be a difficult read for you. But if you are willing to put your biased opinion aside and get to know the generation the world loves to hate, I assure you it will be an exciting and educational ride.

As we all may know, many from previous generations tend to call millennials lazy, which is very hurtful. Okay. Not really, but nonetheless, many tend to feel that way. Therefore, we must take some time to discuss this and figure out why. According to Merriam-Webster, the term "lazy" is defined as "disinclined to activity or exertion. Not energetic or vigorous." So then why are millennials so-called lazy? Millennials have had the luxury of growing up in a world of convenience and instant access to most things.

The Internet has paved the way to things such as online shopping, which is great by the way, plus, other great companies such as Grubhub, UberEATS, and Postmates. These things tend to simplify life for the average millennial, but I don't think they contribute to our so-called laziness. They just make things more convenient in a world of technology and innovation. Hey, at one point in time, people thought newspapers and snail mail were the greatest things since sliced bread.

If lazy is a lack of exertion and activity, then why are millennials lazy? Again, millennials are those born between the 1980s and 1990s. So, I think it is safe to say they more than likely have jobs, go to school, or may even be entrepreneurs. Are millennials doing anything different from anyone from one of the previous generations? I mean, what do you all want from us? Are we supposed to chop trees and build log cabins? I am really starting to think you guys just want us to do whatever you say and to shut up while doing it, but that's just my two rusty pennies.

MILLENNIALS

Many also say that millennials are entitled. So, again we will turn to Merriam-Webster where "entitled" is defined as "having a certain right to benefits and privileges." Not too sure what rights and privileges millennials are receiving that any other person isn't receiving, but again, they just hate because they ain't us. I think it was around 2015 or 2016 that Rico Richie said, "if you ain't got no haters, you ain't popping."

The only things I think most millennials have been entitled to are a very expensive college degree and unemployment. So, if that is what's being referred to, then you all can have that back because we did not sign up to be overeducated, over-qualified, broke people, especially in a world and a country where education was heavily pushed onto our generation. Sounds like a jack move to me, a move to put millennials in debt and destroy our ability to generate any wealth.

I once had a conversation with a guy who's a Gen Xer. Yes, I just wrote "Gen Xer", but as I stated earlier, this isn't necessarily a book to test my level of understanding in the use of grammar and proper English; rather it is something for the people, by the people. The people being millennials, and well it's just little ole me who's doing the writing; but I'm sure my fellow millennials will be picking up what I'm putting down. Man, talking about going off on a tangent! Anyway, so during this conversation, the gentleman stated that "millennials think that because they have a degree, they should start higher up the totem pole. When someone like me who has years of experience had to work my way up." I'm mocking this guy's voice in my head, I wish you all could hear it.

I guess you can say that's a feeling of entitlement, but um, yeah, so if you spent most of your adult life in college, you would want a job that would at least pay you enough to pay back the down payment for a house that you spent on a (degree) piece of paper. Instead most millennials are flipping burgers, serving drinks, or holding down the cash register at Walmart. Most jobs that we feel that we qualify for based on education now require so much experience along with the degree that most millennials were still riding bikes and having sleep overs when they should've been working.

Millennials have been dealt a bad hand and then are being told how they should play that hand by generations of people who still are trying to figure out what "lmbo" and "hashtag" mean. Many millennials are stuck with internships and volunteering free time just to gain experience for most jobs only to still have to compete with every other millennial who has been to college because we were told that's the thing to do.

Then there's the N-word, and no, not the word that some people like to call Blacks or that we use subconsciously in our communities, but narcissistic, which is defined as "extremely self-centered with an exaggerated sense of self-importance. Marked by or characteristic of excessive admiration of or infatuation with oneself." Bet that was a mouthful, but that's what a portion of the population thinks about millennials.

MILLENNIALS

Whatever happened to being able to take pride in what you've accomplished and to get a little recognition for it? If you were part of the MOST educated generation on the planet but also the most underemployed, wouldn't you be a bit self-centered? Yes, we feel like we should start mid-level because most of us have spent four or more years in college. Yes, we want to have days off and not have to work very physically demanding jobs. Therefore, I spent $50,000 on an education so I could put on a collared shirt and some slacks and eat almonds while I type on my keyboard.

We're not responsible for you having to work in the steel mill or work your way up the corporate ladder. We are not the ones who inflated the dollar, drove up the cost of living, and increased college cost. Again, a hand you all dealt but want to tell us how to play. But, guess what? We don't like following your rules.

There is nothing wrong with wanting the work you do to have meaning. Not just because someone decided they would charge you for water to get rich, so you must work to pay for it. Don't get me wrong; I have no problem with capitalism or entrepreneurship. I just have a problem with greed. There is also nothing wrong with a little positive reinforcement and a "good job" here and there. I guess the older generations didn't spend much time developing an understanding of Maslow's Hierarchy of Needs, which, according to S. A. McLeod (2007), states that "people are motivated to achieve certain needs. When one need is fulfilled a person seeks to fulfill the next one, and so on."

Therefore, if you feel as if your basic needs aren't being met, then it is hard to have the desire to seek to meet other needs. To spend most of your life in school, possibly working part-time, only to be a twenty-something-year-old who's either unemployed or underemployed can really hurt your drive and decrease your level of motivation. Trust me, I know. I remember being twenty-four years old and fresh out of the U.S. Navy. I spent the next three years unemployed and attending college. That was a very financially rough and a depressing time.

I remember being in class, and we had an assignment to write a paper on what dream job we all wanted. I will be honest and state that I do not have the dream job that I wrote about, but I have no complaints. Plus, life isn't over, and there's plenty time to get there.

Anyway, one student with whom I had developed a good relationship and who was also a vet was training to be a police officer. He decided not to complete the assignment. When I asked him why, he stated, "I don't have time to spend writing about a dream job when I have bills and a family. I need a real job, I'm not worried about some damn dream job." That really bothered me that day because society and maybe pressure from the millennial stereotypes had driven him to stop dreaming and believing.

In my opinion, there isn't a feeling worse than getting up every day and going to a dead-end job just to survive. My first job after my three years of unemployment was just that. Imagine a twenty-seven-year-old who is college-educated with a nearly three-year-old son trying to live off $8 an hour. I'm sure some will read those last couple of sentences and say, "This is what we mean when we say millennials are entitled." But, let's be realistic. Where in America can you provide for yourself and your family off $8 an hour?

Just because members of previous generations may have done it or didn't have a problem with it doesn't make it okay. These are the types of things we complain about. It's not that we don't want to work or are lazy. We just want a fair chance to compete and provide a life for ourselves. Especially if one has a ton of student loan debt to pay, that humbling $8 an hour just isn't going to cut it.

At the end of the day, millennials just want to be heard and given an opportunity to flourish, especially in a world and economy that we didn't have a hand in creating. The oldest millennial as of the current year is or will be turning forty years old. I don't know everything, but I do know that most people still haven't gotten it together by forty. For those who have, congratulations, but there are many twenty- and thirty-year-olds who, instead of being called lazy, entitled, and narcissistic, are in serious need of guidance and mentorship. Since baby boomers and Gen Xers have it all figured out, remember the old saying "each one teach one"?

Besides, as I stated before, what did the Greatest Generation say about the baby boomers? And what did the baby boomers say about Generation X? Let's not act like you all didn't have flaws and setbacks. Once given the opportunity to prove ourselves, we always do. Anyway, as we progress through this book, we attempt to dissect and discuss some of the things that have hindered and have given the illusion that millennials aren't doing what's necessary to survive in some of the toughest times while dealing with the increasing cost of living, the death of Social Security, and the rising cost of education.

I like to think of millennials as the prototype-generation that shifted the way the world looks at education, company structure, and how work is defined. As we work our way through this information, we will discuss many things about millennials. Some of it may be controversial, and to be honest, I will be taking every chance that I get to hit previous generations with a cheap shot. So, if you are sensitive or not really into us millennial folks, I thank you in advance for at least grabbing a copy.

Because it may get a bit ugly. Not really, I will do my best to make this a worthwhile read. Someone must have millennials' backs in this cold world. We're just a bunch of young people trying to find our way through life like many of you older folks were at one point in time in your lives. So tough it out, and maybe when it's all said and done, we'll all leave with some new information and find someone else to pick on.

Besides reading is good for you, and having a little humor and millennial razzle dazzle to it will make it that much more interesting. In fact, I am willing to bet that after reading this, you will never look at millennials the same. Not only that, you won't mistake them for Generation Z like most people do. For some reason, "millennial" has become the broad term for all young people, which slightly bothers me because I don't think anyone from previous generations would like us calling them all grandparents when we refer to anyone over the age of forty.

There was a time when I thought forty was old. I can vividly remember my grandparents being in their forties, and they were so old to me when, in fact, they weren't. Anyway, I am not sure if someone in his or her mid-thirties likes to be compared to someone who is twenty years old, which is pretty much what most people do when they use the term "millennial" when these two people are not in the same generation.

CHAPTER 2

The Brokest Generation

MILLENNIALS

You would only imagine that after being called lazy, narcissistic, and entitled that life and those old folks from previous generations would so kindly take their foot off the average millennial's neck. But, nope, that's not enough. Life looked that millennial dead in the eye and caught 'em with a clean right hook, then stood over 'em like Muhammad Ali did Sonny Liston in his famous 1965 fight and photo. Most millennials might not know what I am referring to, but that's okay.

Millennials tend to be in a continuous state of zombie-like routines: wake up, go to work, come home, turn on Netflix, pass out, and wake up and do it all over again just to get to those wonderful two days that fall at the end of the week so that we may drink, party, binge on TV, and then have a massive heart attack on Sunday night. We hate that it seems like Monday was just hiding behind the door, waiting to jump out and—in the words of my grandmother—"slap the cowboy piss out of you!"

So then one must ask why are millennials always getting hit with the big end of the stick? We work our butts off, in our own way of course, but nonetheless we work our butts off. Yet, it's still not enough to be self-sufficient for most millennials. Some studies have shown that a large percentage of young people still live at home and depend on their parents for help. Still, nobody has taken a deep look at why. It's like someone cut open an artery, put a band aid on it, then got mad because the person's dying, and they aren't doing anything to save themselves. No one has attempted to stop the bleeding.

23

We cannot hold millennials accountable for the bleeding. Again, the oldest millennial is barely forty years old. In the land of capitalism, greed, corporations, a rising cost of living, inflation, increased costs of education, and expensive healthcare, no one has ever said "Hey, let's make sure we leave the next generation a fighting chance." Instead, we'll do whatever we want and leave it up to them because we'll all be old or dead. But we will still blame them for it.

Everyone seems to be so hellbent on telling millennials how they should live, what type of work ethic to have, and to stop seeking recognition for hard work. Yet, no one has done anything to improve the economic issues the world is facing. We all have had the mantra "go to school and get a good job" programmed into our minds. So, we did just that, Generation Y, aka millennials, are currently the most educated generation alive. Most of those educated people are working jobs that are barely paying enough to make rent, let alone help pay back the expensive education they received.

According to Ferro (2019), "a 2018 survey of 600 Millennials found that the average debt load was $42,000." Please help me understand how someone fresh out of college with very little work experience and a job that pays $10 to $15 an hour has enough to cover rent, utilities, and other expenses such as gas and vehicle maintenance. Is that enough to create a life, and oh yes, we have not added the student loan bill along with maybe some credit card debt.

Then some smart person decided to make the playing field even worse. Your typical young person graduates from college with a bachelor's degree, ready to take on the world, so he goes out and applies for the "good job" that he didn't qualify for with just a high school diploma. But, guess what, young lad! You don't have enough experience. Reminds me of the guy I mentioned earlier who pretty much said, "Screw your education; I worked my way up, and you should do the same." I said that in his voice also.

Anyway, I digress. So, the only option left for most young people who do not want to flip burgers is to apply for internships and volunteer work. Please don't get me wrong; I have no problem with internships. In fact, interning is a good thing for those who may be working toward degrees in specialized fields. In my humble opinion, though, working towards a degree and staying on top of your studies is enough work—not to mention if you may have to work part-time just to pay for school and make ends meet.

Some may read the last paragraph and say, "Typical of a millennial—always complaining and feeling entitled." Yeah, yeah, so what? All I'm saying is the average young person is juggling a lot already. Plus, we are under the constant microscope of old folks who are patiently waiting for a chance to pounce and tell us all about how they had it in their day when they had penny candy and Atari. Yes, that was a cheap shot, and yes, I will be taking those here and there throughout this book.

In the words of Kanye West (2007), "Old folks talking 'bout, back in my day, but homie this is my day. Class started two hours ago, oh am I late? No, I already graduated." This is one of my favorite songs, by the way. Like most millennials who have already graduated, we just want a fair shot at life and the job market along with a chance to build and live and show the world that if they had our hands, they'd chop theirs off. I am sure that when the time comes, we will be doing the same to the generations that follow us, but I do hope that we aren't calling them a bunch of names like our parents and grandparents do to us.

I personally urge all millennials and those following closely behind millennials to learn trades to go along with their fancy college degrees. This way, they can create a side-hustle and open their own businesses to help deal with the current economy and job market. In fact, all people should have a few hustles and different sources of income. That's just my worthless opinion, but it does allow wiggle room and helps in creating wealth and financial freedom. I also suggest that young people take care of their health and get some type of life insurance, but those are some things we will discuss in a later chapter.

Never feel that professions such as electricians, plumbers, and janitors are beneath you or are unimportant fields, especially when you are the boss or are self-employed. According to ZipRecruiter, a market-place for job seekers and employers, the average self-employed electrician earns on average $78,236 a year, and a master plumber earns $59,742 a year. I am not sure about anyone else, but that's a good start and a lot better than waiting tables for tips. Again, that's just my two pennies.

Then why are millennials having such a hard time getting ahead when there are trades and professions out there that pay these livable salaries? Before we go any further, I want to make sure that I protect myself from any legal action and also let you know that I am not a financial expert. But I would like to share a few things on why I think millennials are behind and constantly under fire. Are we clear? Okay, good; let's keep it moving. Ferro (2019) also states that "millennials have less wealth than older generations did at the same age. The median net worth of a Millennial-headed household in 2016 was only $12,500, while Gen X households had a median net worth of $15,100 when that cohort was in the 20- to 35-year-old age range."

One reason I think that this may be the case has to be inflation and cost of living. According to Merriam-Webster, "inflation" is defined as "a continuing rise in the general price level usually contributed to an increase in the volume of money and credit relative to available goods and services." In a nutshell, the price of things keeps increasing, but the value of money is decreasing because in America, we print money; and the more we print, the less it is worth. Inflation is something that happens, and you and I have no control over that; but we must educate ourselves and older generations, whom I think it's safe to assume, know that things cost a lot more, especially in comparison to when they were the age of the average millennial.

In a recent blog post titled "How to Beat Inflation," Curry (2020) states that "Currently, the annual rate of inflation is 2.1%, according to the latest Consumer Price Index (CPI). At time of writing, the national rate for a savings account held at a deposit institution is 0.09% APY, while the average return on certificates of deposit (CDs) is around .13% to .98%, according to the FDIC." So, based on this information, the average millennial is fighting a constant uphill battle. If money is losing its value quicker than the money you save gains interest, how do you expect people to win?

I was once told by someone, not quite sure who, but he said that "money is a currency and much like a river it should be moving. It's worthless if it's sitting still." So, if we are losing money quicker than we can save it, we need to look to some different investment options. Again, I am no expert, and most older people are still teaching us old methods. Then we are up you-know-what's creek without a paddle. Millennials are constantly being bashed, and if you ask me, we are the most hated generation ever.

Then why isn't someone educating us on ways to save and create wealth that isn't being eaten by inflation? Instead, we just go to college and then enter the job pool to compete against Lord knows how many other and maybe more qualified candidates. As I mentioned, I am no expert, so please don't read this and then go out and make any decisions and hold me accountable. Please seek expert financial advice. I personally think that millennials should begin to investigate buying land and real estate. We all know that they are not making any more land, and people will always need a place to live.

Debt is the new slavery, and I personally feel that this was by design and not by chance. I keep touching on debt, especially student debt, because Generation Y is the generation that was pushed toward education. This led to a rise in for-profit institutions that charge extremely high tuition and book fees. Some even only allow you to purchase certain books from certain providers, which are very expensive. This may have something to do with the Great Recession, but again, millennials are too young to have had anything to do with that; but I am sure they would like to blame them.

According to Chappelow (2009), "the Great Recession is a term that represents the sharp decline in economic activity during the late 2000s. This period is considered the most significant downturn since the Great Depression. The economic slump began when the U.S. housing market went from boom to bust, and large amounts of mortgage-backed securities (MBS's) and derivatives lost significant value." Not sure about any other millennials, but during this time, I was about twenty-four-years-old. I also come from a single-parent home in poverty, so we didn't own a home or have a mortgage.

So, why do we get so much heat for just being who we are when we inherited a world and economy that we had no part in destroying, yet everything is always our fault? We want recognition for our work, entitled; we want to have flexible work schedules, lazy; we think we are the sugar-honey-iced-tea, narcissistic. Man, in the words of my aunt, "if it wasn't for bad luck, we wouldn't have any luck at all."

Therefore, when are we going to get our chance to be great without being called a bunch of names? In the words of the late, great Tupac Shakur (1993) "And don't blame me—I was given this world, I didn't make it." But I genuinely don't think that most people from previous generations see it that way. They just want millennials to shut up and do whatever they say because their way is the right way, right?

I am sure we all know that that is not the case because they have their flaws. So, then the question is why are millennials so broke and behind financially? A lot of that has to do with the rising cost of education and inflation. We continue to put our best foot forward and work hard, but it just isn't enough. It's like taking two steps forward and one step back. The average millennial is drowning in student loan debt with no idea how to get through it. Is this the result of circumstances or the lack of a solid foundation to build on?

Millennials inherited a house with its foundation built on sand on the side of a cliff that experiences twelve-foot tides every hour. I may be over-exaggerating, but that's just how I see it. So, maybe that's just my narcissistic, millennial thinking. Oh well, who cares? Old folks can tell it their way in their book. Anyway, if we inherited a house we didn't build, then what are we going to do to fix it up?

Don't get me wrong. If I left my kid a house, I would feel some type of way if he complained too, but I would also understand his concerns about the roof, foundation, and value of the home. So why aren't millennials given the courtesy of complaining about the piece of crap house we inherited with understanding ears instead of egotistical previous generations being so uptight about it? I suggest that no one wants to be criticized for the work they have done. Sound familiar Gen X and baby boomers? I am sure it doesn't, but that's okay. That's just cognitive dissonance, and it's been well studied. Yes, I took another shot, so keep your guard up. I've got hands for days.

MILLENNIALS

Talk about having it rough, that's the only thing young people were taught, which would help them build a life, purchase a home, and start a family. You know, all that American Dream stuff is costing so much money you have one of the brokest generations ever. Yet, everyone looks over this and just points the finger at millennials. Can I have the day off? Oh, you're lazy. Yeah, right! I am stressed out and going crazy because I have a huge debt shackled to my ankle, and I haven't even found a decent job that'll pay me enough to get out of debt. Millennial life is stressful, and I am surprised we're not all alcoholics.

Now that I said that, I wouldn't be surprised if we get blamed every time someone's favorite wine is out of stock. Okay, I really must stop taking cheap shots, but this might be my only chance. I mean, what's the worst that can happen? Some Gen Xer or boomer reads this and slanders me? Not really concerned—I am here for us millennials, and we've got something to say. Besides, I've heard so much about millennials that I am numb to the derogatory insults.

Anyway, I personally feel that there should be some sort of balance. I mean, if you leave college with $30,000 in debt, for example, then you should at least be able to find employment that pays enough to counter that debt. Yes, I know that just sounded entitled, but, I mean, how do you all expect young folks to get ahead? I am sure that back in your day, you all didn't complain, ate fire, and raised bees with no protective gear. But you also didn't have to pay an arm, leg, and kidney for a decent education. Work with us for Pete's sake! We are just young people trying to make a living in a world that forgot we were just young kids during a tremendous shift in this country and the world.

I know I continue to kick a dead horse, but I really want to drive this home. Debt is killing us, and I somewhat blame our elders because the young folks were depending on you all to be a source of guidance and information. Instead, you taught us old tactics that are fading away, and then got mad at us for needing help. Needing help and feeling entitled are not the same. It isn't that young people want to have something for nothing, it's that they want to feel as if the years they spent pursuing an education would pay off.

There is nothing fulfilling or motivating about being college-educated and having to wait tables. No offense to anyone who waits table because the bills do not stop, and you must do what you must do. In the military, we had a saying, "Rank has its privileges," so all I'm saying is someone who put in the hard work and dedication it takes to complete higher education should be able to begin a little ahead of waiting tables, unless that's just what they want to do or maybe use as a part-time source of income.

As I said, though, nothing toward anyone who does what they must do to pay the bills no matter if it's waiting tables or making tables. I just think that the point of getting a higher education is so that you can move into a more corporate, white-collar job. Cheers to the brokest generation! The term "millennial" has become a derogative term old people use to define all young people. In fact, I heard people who are clearly millennials bagging on millennials. Once educated on the fact that they are millennials themselves, their response is usually something like, "Well, I'm Gen X-minded." Are you, though? You're probably swimming in college debt like the rest of us, cohabitating, or working a dead-end job.

Instead of using the word "millennial" whenever you want to refer to a young person, which, by the way, most of you are usually wrong, and the person you are referring to is probably Generation Z, you should start saying "young, in debt up to their neck's hustlers, who, for some reason, still seem to be living their best lives. Kid- and mortgage-free, well not because they probably want to but because it costs too much. Despite that, still hardcore little bad-asses with a knack for getting shit done." Please pardon my language, in fact, screw that, don't pardon it. I'm a millennial!

CHAPTER 3

Turn a Blind Eye

MILLENNIALS

As we continue, we will begin to shed light on a few things that most people either don't know or don't care to know. Contrary to popular belief, millennials are leading the pack in a few areas. This, alone, should help those who criticize to gather a better understanding and, hopefully, some respect for the work that millennials put in. If not, then it would be safe to conclude that they just like picking on young people even though we are dedicated to education and self-improvement.

I used to get so upset when I would hear people speak badly about millennials until one day, I realized most people are misinformed about millennials. They don't know how old millennials are, and they don't know much about our characteristics and traits. I've sat in pubs and various other settings and have watched older people talk trash about some nineteen- or twenty-year-old up to the point when I had to butt in and let them know the age range. It's almost as if "millennials" has become a derogatory term for all young people, which is sad because ignorance is not bliss in this case.

If you are going to bad-mouth somebody, at least have your facts straight. Please do not group us with Generation Z. They have their own set of flaws, and as messed up as it may seem, I hope they get bad-mouthed too. Then again, no I don't, those young people just want a chance to be great like millennials want their chance. It's hard to be young as if we all had something to do with it when we were born.

Not to sound cocky, but you know what, screw it. To be cocky, many millennials would have been superstars in whatever they chose had they been born earlier.

Not to toot our own horns, but millennials are the shit. Plain and simple, no ifs, ands, or buts about it. We were born during a time of turmoil yet opportunity.

All millennials did was play the hand they were dealt. They were creative and forward-thinking. They saw a need for change and improvement and voiced their opinions about it. Instead of calling them entitled, they should be called bold, fearless, and innovative. But everyone is upset because they don't follow the rules and did a good job seeing through the BS. The economy changed, corporate structure changed, and they changed along with it.

That's okay, though, because we will spend some time educating the masses about the world's most hated generation. Hopefully, when we are done, more people will understand the uphill battle that most young people are fighting. Not only is it uphill, it's muddy, eroding, and everyone is wearing flip flops. That may be a bit exaggerated, but life is hard for young people; and the world needs to understand that. Most of them are not lazy or entitled; they are just weighed down with a lot of issues involving debt and a poor economy.

Contrary to popular belief, millennials are just as loyal to their employers as are any other generation. Yeah, I know that may have left a lot of you taken aback, but it's very true. Many consider millennials to be job-hoppers, yet that's not the case. In my opinion, they don't have the luxury to job-hop. Finding a job is enough trouble, so to think that one could just jump from job to job is a bit farfetched. Job-hop if you want, and you may be homeless and a beggar.

MILLENNIALS

According to an article in the Wall Street Journal (Dill, 2020), "In January 2018, 70% of workers between the ages of 22 and 37, commonly known as the millennial generation, had worked for their current employer for 13 months or more, according to an analysis of federal data by the Pew Research Center. By comparison, that number was 69% for workers who were in the same age group in 2002 and are known as Generation X." So, if millennials in comparison to Generation X at the same age during that time are no different, then why are they considered job-hoppers?

I have a few ideas why this may be the case would you all would like to hear. Maybe because someone met a handful of millennials who may have job-hopped. Or someone may have worked with a millennial on whom he based his entire opinion about millennials. Or someone may have millennial family members who are job-hoppers. News flash, though, guys and gals. You can't base your opinion on a few people. If that were the case, we could say all baby boomers were farmers and Gen Xers worked in a manufacturing plant.

I am willing to bet that that statement would ruffle a few feathers, but hey, I know a few people from those generations who worked those professions. Does that give me the right to conclude that all people from those generations were farmers and plant workers? No, it doesn't, so why group all millennials? There is a decent age gap between the oldest millennial and the youngest. Just to shed some light on the age gap, there are a few things I have experienced that some millennials may not have.

DELANO PERRY

I was alive for the phone booth, rotary phones, Nintendo, and dial-up. You could ask the youngest millennial about these things, and they could only tell you stories that they've heard about these ancient, mystical devices. I also was around when TVs were black and white, and they weren't flat. Mm-hmm, that's right, the good ole boob-tube, and hell I was even around when floor model TVs meant you were doing it big. Therefore, we should all come to an understanding that times change, and although some may be in the same generation, they may not have experienced the same world.

I am familiar with MS DOS and Windows 95 and Saturday mornings that consisted of Looney Tunes and revived episodes of School House Rock. The youngest millennial was about one- or two-years-old when School House Rock aired its last episode. Ask them if they know what that show's about, and they probably couldn't tell you. In 1996, I was an eleven-year-old knucklehead living in public housing with a single mother.

Perhaps I might be driving my point too far home, but I just want everyone to be clear on how the age range for not just millennials but for all generations works. You can't say that a twenty-five-year-old and a thirty-five-year-old have the same views on life. I mean, if you are an older reader, think back to when you were twenty-five. I can tell you that despite having been in the Navy and having some college under my belt at that time, I was all kinds of screwed up. In fact, I think I may have been sleeping on my cousin's couch. So, let's not all act like we owned a home and had tons of money stashed away at twenty-five.

MILLENNIALS

Millennials are no different from any other generation. They are just living life according to the environment in which they grew up and in which they currently live. It's just sad that the term "millennial" has become a form of insult because most are misinformed and too stuck in their old ways to learn about the future leaders of the free world.

It is truly a huge slap in the face for millennials to be better educated than previous generations, yet, they are underemployed and constantly criticized. And yes, I know that the counterargument is always experience, but we were taught to focus on education because we were under the impression that this would help reduce some of the experience needed so that we may just be a few steps up on the corporate ladder. I was under the impression that that was the way it used to be, or at least I've heard stories of more experienced workers training their college-educated new supervisors on the job. In fact, the father, who's a baby boomer, of a good friend of mine once quit his job because he had to train his young college-educated new boss. That didn't sit too well with him.

So, if this is the way it used to be, then why are young people locking themselves into so much debt for a system that has been altered? Really how can you expect someone who is fresh out of college to have the degree and five years of experience? Who wants to spend their entire time in college doing internships and volunteering? You all are aware that this is unpaid work in most cases, right? The last time I checked food, gas, and books still cost money.

Millennials may be misunderstood now and low-key hated on by most, but we did manage to take the lead in a few things. One of those things being education—something that we have hit on a few times up to this point, especially regarding cost. Nevertheless, young people are still in hot pursuit of higher education. In a study conducted by the Pew Research Center (Bialik & Fry, 2019), "Today's young adults are much better educated than their grandparents, as the share of young adults with a bachelor's degree or higher has steadily climbed since 1968. Among Millennials, around four-in-ten (39%) of those ages 25 to 37 have a bachelor's degree or higher, compared with just 15% of the Silent Generation, roughly a quarter of Baby Boomers and about three-in-ten Gen Xers (29%) when they were the same age."

Therefore, if millennials are more educated than previous generations and just as loyal to their employers as previous generations, then where does all the shade come from? I can only think of one thing, and I stated it earlier. Most are uptight about millennials because they are rebels and will not just blindly do as they are told without some sort of explanation as to why. One thing I have noticed being a young man who rubs shoulders with quite a few Gen Xers is that they hate to be asked why it's like a slap to the face for them.

When you are confident, smart, and able to analyze things on your own, old folk get upset when you don't do what they tell you to do. I've been told, "You can't tell me nothing," "You think you know everything," "He's so argumentative" and even that people shouldn't listen to or do business with me because of things I believe in like reading books, setting goals, and having dreams are supposedly stupid. That's really something to say, but hey, old folk are sensitive when you don't follow the old "do as I say, not as I do" saying. Besides, that's a weak person who felt inferior. Beta males are always slanderous and untrustworthy.

That's neither here nor there, though the point is millennials are not traditional, and they like to understand why they are doing certain things. If it doesn't make sense or can be improved, then they just don't rock with it. Plain and simple, everyone was sent here to do something great, and when things do not resonate with who you are, then you shouldn't just follow along with it simply because that's the way it's always been done. If we all thought that way, the railroad and steel industries would still rule the world, and it would be okay to use child labor.

In a nutshell, get out of your feelings about millennials because times have changed, and you are too old and too slow to change with them. So, it makes you uncomfortable that millennials operate a little differently in a world and economy that a bunch of old, greedy people screwed up then blamed millennials for not fixing the mess? Yes, we tend to leave the nest later than previous generations, and yes, we don't quite have it figured out. But how can we when it costs an arm, a leg, and two pints of blood to live in the current economy. Plus, the average millennial is drowning in debt before the age of thirty, and most haven't even purchased a home yet.

Does that not sound like a shitty start—to be highly educated, in debt, and fighting for meaningful employment? Despite the deck being stacked against millennials, there's still no doubt in my mind that it will work itself out. I know I may be bagging on previous generations a bit much, but I know that all generations have faced their own set of problems. Yet, look at you—you turned out fine, so millennials will do the same. Tides turn, and economies swing back and forth. But the saying goes, "Tough times don't last, but tough people do." And dammit, millennials are as about as tough as they come.

There are policies and programs being put into place to help with the growing cost of education. Eventually, it will all work out, and millennials just have to be patient, continue to be innovative, and keep our foot on the gas pedal. Education has always played a major part in success and income, so it should never be abandoned. Personally, I just think some people and organizations should stop trying to capitalize on it. In fact, I personally think education should be extremely cheap and possibly free because these are the people who will continue to push the world forward.

What's a world without doctors, lawyers, scientists, engineers, and scholars? If the world needs those who are educated in certain fields, then doesn't it make sense to make that obtainable without having to ruin your credit and buying power before you get a good start at life? This is not to take away from tradesmen and skilled workers because they too are extremely valuable, and their jobs usually require some sort of technical training and education. Besides, you can make a nice life for yourself as I showed earlier with the electrician and plumber examples.

In the chapters that follow, we will discuss a few things such as health, marriage, home ownerships, and retirement. Millennials may not always seem like they have it all together, but we are some savvy folks and are good at making a way out of no way. We are breaking down barriers and shedding light on things such as cohabitation, waiting to have children, and divorce. In a world that may seem at times like it has overlooked millennials and babied Generation Z, millennials are still making things work in our favor.

I am willing to bet that ten to fifteen years from now, the world will have let up on millennials because it will have worked out the kinks. Then we will all just find a way to buy on the following generations. And not to seem so excited, but I can't wait! Just kidding. As I've mentioned before, every generation has its pros and cons. We are all just here trying to figure out this thing called life and, in the process, make a little money and enjoy some of the material things that come along with it.

Yet, many people tend to look the other way or turn a blind eye to the issues that millennials are facing. Of course, it is no one's responsibility to handle anyone else's problems, but at least be aware and understand that they do have their own set of problems—many like the ones previous generations faced and many unlike anything that any generation has faced. Where would I get the nerve to tell someone living during the Great Depression how they should live or to tell someone who dealt with Jim Crow laws and segregation how to live. I mean, as I currently write this book, we are dealing with a pandemic.

Currently, as I write, we are dealing with a novel form of coronavirus better known as COVID-19. This has caused all sorts of issues in the economy. And never in all my life, let alone just a few months ago, would I have thought that many Americans would be out of work, and we would be confined, for the most part, to our homes in order to prevent the spread of a virus that has claimed many lives. Ironically, many baby boomers, Gen Xers, millennials, Generation Zers, and I did not think or know we would be living during this time. Please do not quote me on the "Generation Alpha" name, but I think that may be the current name of the generation following the Tide-Pod-eating and condom-sniffing generation. It may change, but as for now, we will go with that.

By the way, I apologize for taking a shot at Generation Z, but I mean, come on, they mistake many of you as millennials all the time, and it makes us a little upset.

CHAPTER 4

What Worked for You May Not Work for Me

MILLENNIALS

I am sure that it is very clear by now that millennials aren't quite like previous generations. They pursue education more than previous generations, they have more debt, and of course, according to some questionable source, millennials are entitled. I hate to break it to you all, but millennials are setting the pace in a few other areas. They are changing the way the world views some of the traditional stan-dards.

You would find it quite strange that a generation that everyone seems to think is entitled and narcissistic actually prefers peace of mind and purpose more than they do compensation. According to an article by Tredgold (2016), "64 percent of Millennials would rather make $40,000 a year at a job they love than $100,000 a year at a job they think is boring." Not sure about anyone else, but that doesn't give me the impression of someone who is entitled. I see a group of people who understand that money is just a tool, and if managed effectively, that money can allow a person to live an amazing life of purpose and contribution as opposed to participating in the rat race, losing all your hair, and dying from stress because everyone is driven by status and credentials.

Don't get me wrong; I am all for making money and creating financial freedom. But that can be accomplished once you figure out how much is enough for you, and then you can live below your means and make smart investments. I think millennials have developed an understanding of this. Purposeful living always pays more than a few bills made of linen and cotton. Yes, money isn't paper, which is why you can wash it, and it just comes out a little wrinkled. By the way, I am sure I am not the only person who has washed money. Nothing better than finding a few dollars in some jeans. It's like hitting the lottery.

Anyway, let's not get too far off topic because I want to really make sure I hammer this one in. The so-called entitled guys and gals will prefer to work for a lot less money if they enjoy what they are doing. Well, isn't that something? Talk about having your thing on a string. Not sure what that means, but it's a pretty popular saying in the black community.

Honestly, the only point I am trying to make here is that young people, in my opinion, are getting back to the basics by realizing that life and work are much more manageable and peaceful when you're doing what you love. In fact, I am sure that it has been said that if you're doing what you love, you'll never work a day in your life. I cannot speak for anyone else, but I sure am not a fan of work; and I do not know many people who are. So, do what you love, and life will be a breeze.

But that's just the beginning of all the wonderful characteristics of millennials. These are truly some special people. The mold was broken when the Creator made this group of people. In that same article, Tredgold (2016) states that "35 percent of employed Millennials have started their own business on the side to supplement their income." So, it is much easier to take a job you love that may not necessarily pay a very handsome salary, but what does that matter if you've got an entrepreneurial mind?

MILLENNIALS

We are living in a strange time when it comes to the economy, and if I didn't state it plainly earlier, I am a fan of entrepreneurship and the side-hustle. An additional source of income, in my opinion, is not an option but is a necessity. I take my hat off to those who are out there starting and running businesses of their own. It is not easy and not for everyone, trust me I know.

So, I will take this time to let anyone who may be running a business reading this know that I commend you. It is, by far, one of the most stressful journeys you may ever take. If things aren't going well, keep at it, and if things are going well, be a mentor and share the wealth. Whatever you do, don't quit, and don't listen to the naysayers because if it were easy, everyone would be doing it.

Hopefully, I didn't lose any of you who aren't running your own businesses, but I can relate; and maybe someone who was about to give up will read those lines and give it another shot. Anyway, young people are also embracing the fact that one source of income is not enough, but instead of working two jobs, they are building something on the side. This can allow them to create jobs for others plus build something that maybe their kids can be part of one day. This is the key to creating legacy and financial freedom.

Speaking of legacy and children, millennials aren't big fans of having kids or at least having kids right now. And I am sure that if you've read this far, then you can take an educated guess as to why or at least understand one of the reasons many millennials are choosing to either delay having kids or not have them at all. In an article from

Business Insider, Hoffower (2019) states that "1,858 men and women ages 20 to 45—64% said childcare is too expensive, 44% said they can't afford to have more children, and 43% said they waited to have kids because of financial instability."

Debt and finances seem to keep being an issue that millennials have to face. Having and raising kids is never easy, and in my opinion, no matter how much you plan for it, you're never quite ready to deal with the purple crying, changing diapers, teething, and baby puke. Yet, it is a beautiful thing that many millennials may never get to experience because things such as college debt and cost of living are hindering this from happening.

Not sure who remembers, but it went something like "First comes love, then comes marriage, then comes so-and-so with a baby carriage." If not, that's okay, it's an old playground song that we would sing as kids whenever we caught wind that some boy or girl liked someone. The point is that most people tend to date, fall in love, get married, and then have kids. But since many millennials are financially unstable and having kids costs a lot, millennials also delay marriage. In fact, many millennials are shacking-up instead of getting married simply because it is more cost-effective for the struggling young person. Young people, in general, are cohabiting with several other friends and family members. Just to pick at the scab again, this doesn't seem like entitled people to me. People who feel entitled would probably want a place to themselves instead of with a few roommates.

MILLENNIALS

Being that millennials are deciding to marry and start families later than previous generations, many are making the decision to protect what they bring to the table. This delay in marriage gives them more time to obtain things in life. Plus, I know after tackling huge college debt, shacking up with a few buddies, and maxing out a few credit cards, you wouldn't want to lose everything you've built over the years. So, millennials are really taking advantage of prenuptial agreements.

Also, because many millennials have so much student loan debt, they are being mindful of this before going into marriage. So, the prenup is a good tool for this as well. According to CNBC (Dickler, 2018), "Prenups, which safeguard individual assets such as retirement accounts, real estate and investments, can also cover one partner's student loan or credit card debt." This is good because I know I wouldn't want to be responsible for someone else's student loans when I have my own to deal with.

When I think of millennials, I am brought back to my time in the U.S. Navy. During this time, I worked as a Boatswain Mate, and I am not sure if you all are familiar with the term. But that's not important; what's important is that I used to work for a Chief Warrant Officer, and he had his own term for "semper fi," short for *semper fidelis*, the Marine Corps' motto, which is Latin for "always faithful or always loyal." The Warrant Officer, who we called the ship's Bos'n, would always say "semper Gumby," which he translated as "always flexible," because millennials are always flexible and adapt well to any situation.

This is a very special group of young people, and the fact that despite swimming in debt and being behind previous generations at the same age, they are finding creative ways to survive during some very trying times. The fact that young people are taking their time with having kids and starting families is contributing to a few other statistics that previous generations have viewed differently from how they do. Cohabiting has its advantages, and young people are using this opportunity to save money and lower divorce rates.

Divorce can be very testy situations and, at times, end terribly. Although it may sometimes be the best solution for those whose marriages just aren't working, they can have lasting effects on children who may be involved and can lead to financial devastation. I once heard someone say that their reason for not marrying was because some of the most financially devastating events they have ever witnessed were not failed businesses or bankruptcy but were divorce.

Luckily for young people, they may not have to experience this because they are doing a good job at keeping the statistics low. In fact, Eickmeyer (2015) says, "At least seven out of ten men and women with cohabitation experience report that cohabitation may help divorce-proof marriages." So, the fact that some millennials are cohabiting with their current significant other just to get by may help build a better bond when and if those individuals ever decide to jump the broom.

Millennials are known for shaking things up, and to be honest, I think that's why most people feel the way they feel about them. People tend to not like change, and millennials have changed corporate cultures, living situations, and marriage. But we all know that one doesn't just wake up one day married. There are usually events that lead up to marriage, one being dating. And if you guessed it, then you are right. Millennials have played a part in changing the dating world.

With the rise of dating sites and apps such as Tinder, dating isn't as traditional as it once was, although Tinder has an iffy reputation. I personally have no experience with the dating app, but I have heard stories from some interesting people. Believe it or not, even though young people are known for hook-ups, they are not as sexually active as previous generations at the same age. There are several expert opinions as to why this may be the case, but that's for another day.

As crazy as it may sound, because older people think all young people do is listen to terrible music, play video games, and have sex, according to Parker-Pope (2019), "A 2017 study in the Archives of Sexual Behavior found that many younger millennials in their early 20s aren't having sex, and are more than twice as likely to be sexually inactive than the previous generation." Now part of that may be from younger people sitting home and playing video games for hours, but that's a matter of opinion. I personally think that young people view sex and marriage differently than previous generations.

At the end of the day, life and times are changing, and there's a saying that goes "the only thing constant in life is change." Hey, at one point, people were farmers and sharecroppers, wives were stay-at-home moms, and wearing seatbelts was optional. Well, at least I thought it was optional because we never wore them as kids. At times, when we would all pile up in the car, there would be a kid sitting on the armrest between the driver and passenger. As some would say, "Those were the good ole days."

I got a bit off topic there, so let's get back to enlightening the world about the greatest generation, just my opinion. Thus far, we have shed light on the fact that millennials are all about cohabitation, marrying later in life, staying married, entrepreneurship, and not engaging in much sex. It seems to me that young people aren't just entitled but have some pretty good morals and values. Speaking of morals and values, though it may come as a surprise, young people are not big on organized religions.

In fact, young people aren't religious at all. There are many reasons why that may be, but we don't want to dive that deep. We just want to draw a little attention to the fact that religion isn't as big with young people as it may have been with previous generations. Besides, religion can be a touchy subject, and I am not here to judge what anyone chooses to believe. I will say that some thought it was maybe just a phase, but according to a 2019 article by Cox and Thomson-DeVeaux, "there's mounting evidence that today's younger genera-tions may be leaving religion for good."

This may be the fact that millennial parents weren't very committed to religious practices, so young people weren't exposed to it in their households. I personally wasn't raised by a mother who was religious, but my grandparents were. In fact, my grandfather would get up Sunday mornings and spend the morning getting dressed and listening to gospel music. To be honest, I hated it because he would not allow us to watch TV, so we spent our time outside mostly just so we wouldn't have to listen to that music. Terrible, right? Although I had very Christian grandparents and family members as I got older, I strayed further and further away from religion.

For reasons that we will not discuss, I have very solid reasons, and no one has been able to alter them. As I stated, though many people weren't raising their children the way my grandparents were raised, religion wasn't part of the foundation. Nevertheless, millennials didn't turn out too bad—well except for being entitled, you know. Hopefully, you picked up on my sarcasm because I don't like that entitled label or people who bad-mouth us millennials. Unlike a lot of people, I believe in my generation.

I personally didn't turn towards religion as I got older, but maybe some young people will. Sometimes after people get a few life experiences and start families of their own, they may tend to make religion a part of their family foundation, or maybe they will meet a partner who may be religious and that may draw them toward a religious faith. I have friends who have married and converted to their partner's religious beliefs, so it's never too late.

Religion has been the foundation for many families for years. I do not think that religion has been completely forgotten; it's just that times are changing, and people are finding their own ways to deal with the trials and tribulations that come with life. I have heard quite a few times from several different people and sources that we are spiritual beings having a human experience. Rather than human beings having a spiritual experience, in my opinion, people are tapping into that spirituality more than they are following organized religions. There is surely nothing wrong with this. In fact, it is somewhat of a religion.

You can search online on nearly every social media outlet and find out how popular spirituality is becoming. If you ask me, most religions have a touch of spirituality within them. So, I guess people decided they could have a relationship with their God or higher power, whichever you prefer, without the religious component. Now before people want to start beating me up online and possibly in person, I am just speaking on the things I witness myself, not as a whole. I do not want to offend anyone or come off as someone who is making this about religion. I'm just speaking from personal experience, which is limited.

CHAPTER 5

Drunk, Depressed, and Dying

MILLENNIALS

I was skeptical about this chapter, but I truly feel that there are a few things we should discuss. I have spent time trash-talking previous generations while defending my own generation—not because this is about trying to convince anyone to take sides or to create some generational feuds but because I just wanted everyone to have some knowledge about the things that millennials are facing. A few major things that young people face are drug and alcohol abuse, depression, and unhealthy habits.

I know that every generation has faced its issues, but this is one that is near and dear to me. Mental illness and addiction are nothing to take lightly. This generation is in crisis, and there are several contributing factors. I have joked and have done a little trash-talking up to this point, but here I will do my best to keep it professional simply because I want any and everyone who is reading this who may be fighting a silent battle to know that I understand. I know how you feel, especially being someone who has been diagnosed with Post Traumatic Stress Disorder and moderate Major Depression Disorder. And not to take away from anyone else's situation, but we black Americans are rarely ever afforded the opportunity to have mental illnesses.

We are often misdiagnosed or simply misunderstood. I won't spend much time on that or make this something about race. Again, this is just to shed light on the situation that young adults are facing. And we need to understand a few of the contributing reasons why this may be so. Being labeled lazy, narcissistic, entitled, or crybabies doesn't compare to this issue that is affecting an entire generation.

Just to help put this into perspective, in recent years, we have had quite a few people in the entertainment industry who were young adults lose their lives way too soon because of drugs and alcohol. I am sure most young people reading this know most of these names. Some of you older people may not, but that's okay, I just wanted to mention a few people who had big plans, were on their way to greatness, and left too soon. I do not know any of these people personally, so I will not speak too much on them out of respect.

In recent years, we lost great people who had made an impact on the world and were way too young to pass on, such as Amy Winehouse, Lil Peep, Mac Miller, and Juice WRLD. Those are just to name a few, but I could name many more whom we have lost in the black community to prescription cough syrup and pills. Young people are struggling and dealing with a lot of underlying problems. Now who's to say where this all stems from, but nevertheless, it needs to be addressed.

Along with the rise of drug and alcohol addiction, many young people are overwhelmed with the everyday struggles of life so much so that many of them have committed suicide. Now I will not sit here and act as if I have all the answers or as if I don't have problems of my own because believe me; I do, and the Department of Veteran Affairs has extended all its resources to me. For those who are less fortunate to have outlets and resources at their disposal, suicide rates have risen. This is a permanent solution to temporary problems. And why are so many of us missing the signs and cries for help? Young people, you are needed and have much to offer to the world.

MILLENNIALS

Although I did mention a few celebrities, that was not to overshadow those who are not "famous," and I put that in quotations because I do not think fame is a real thing. Anyway, we sometimes forget those who deal with things every day that aren't on TV or radio. This, in my opinion, makes it harder for those people as it can lead to depression and feelings of worthlessness. Much of this could be prevented if we all developed a little more compassion and understanding for one another. Also, we should stop shaming people for being different and for dealing with things differently.

There have been a few slightly unbelievable statistics over the past few years. According to a *WebMD* article (Thompson, 2019), "During the past decade, drug-related deaths among that age group increased by 108%, alcohol-induced deaths by 69%, and suicides by 35%, according to the report from the Trust for America's Health and Well Being Trust." That same article also states that "[o]pioid overdose death rates among millennials increased by more than 500% between 1999 and 2017, and deaths caused by synthetic opioids increased by a staggering 6,000%." If this doesn't make you take a few moments to reflect, then I don't know what will.

Six thousand percent, wow, I can't think of anything that I would want to see increase that much except for maybe my investments and bank account. This should be raising all the red flags and setting off all the alarms. Instead, everyone is more focused on the fact that we want time off and want to be recognized for doing a good job. Millennials are the children and grandchildren of baby boomers and Generation X, so why aren't they concerned?

This is something that many people from previous generations may not be too familiar with, so I can understand if they may not understand how serious it is. But it is up to us millennials to stick together and provide support for one another. I know that life can sometimes get hectic, and we get wrapped up in a world of smartphones and information, but we must check up on each other and be there when we can.

Mental illness is not something that should be laughed about, and no one should have to feel ashamed for dealing with mental health. I know for a fact if 10 years ago I had said to one of my friends or family members that I was having issues, they would have had all the wrong things to say and would have tried and make me feel "crazy." It took years of reflection, getting to know myself, and some therapy to say screw everybody and to admit and accept that I had issues and needed help.

There is nothing wrong with admitting that you need help. Life is an interesting journey, and it takes many years to develop some sort of understanding. I can honestly say that 90 percent of the time I have no clue what I am doing. I go "crazy" on the inside all the time while putting on a smile that may not be real until I must go into hiding for weeks at a time. Even with help, and at one point, medication, it still isn't easy. But there is no need for me and any other young person to feel that we need to run to drugs and alcohol to cope.

These things may feel good in the moment, but once they wear off, the problem is still there. All the while, the only thing you have done to yourself is damage your organs and body. There are lots of programs and services available for those who may need help dealing with mental illness, depression, and addiction. Don't be ashamed to get the help you need. Hell, they already call us entitled, you may as well be entitled to help yourself.

Help yourself to a peace of mind and the things you need so you can take back control over your life. Millennials are, in my opinion, living in some of the best times in history. But because we have access to so much information and convenience in the palms of our hands, it has become sensory overload, and too much of anything, regardless of what it is, can be bad. It may be a little-known fact but drinking too much water can be a bad thing. Yep, that's right! Too much water can lead to what is called water intoxication.

Crazy, right? Water intoxication is when too much water in the body causes electrolyte imbalance and reduces the sodium in the body to a dangerously low level. Having so much technology and access makes the world smaller, and because we are swimming in a pool of luxury, we have become too numb to some of the things that make life what it is and make humans what they are. We use Instagram "likes" and social media for validation at times, and this creates a false reality—makeup, cars, clothes, and popularity. But once you remove the television, internet, and all the "matrix" components, real life can be kind of boring.

The key to helping young people battle this alarming issue is to bring awareness to the situation. Much like any other issue the world faces, making people aware of things such as causes, triggers, and treatment options helps those who may not understand things like mental illness be of better service to those who are suffering, and millennials are suffering. I know those from previous generations may not be Facebook-savvy or know how to work a smartphone, but they are very smart people; and if we educate them enough—much like my purpose for this book—then perhaps they will look past our "entitled" personalities and be able to pick up on the early warning signs of things like depression and addiction. That way, they may also pick up on the signs that could lead to bodily harm and even worse, suicide. Fellow millennials, your help is needed as well, so let's stop shaming and bullying others who may need your help.

Mental illnesses such as depression and, ultimately, suicide are terrible things. And if I've taken you too deep, please bear with me. I tried to step this down as we moved through reading. But those things, which are sad of course, are just a few things with which millennials are dealing. Now before I move further, please don't think that I am blaming anyone from other generations. I am just asking for understanding and am attempting to raise awareness.

But millennials are facing a few other monsters—one of them being obesity. Trust me, though I was in the military, and as a guy who's only 5' 6", I can say that sometimes the BMI scale is a bit annoying. In my younger days, speaking as if I am old, I was about 140 pounds, and if memory serves me correct, I wasn't supposed to be much over 155 pounds. Now I was skinny as ever, but I had a bit of muscle. And no, I am not exaggerating, I have pictures to prove it. I would, at times, be on the border of overweight or obese due to my height.

So, I would often have to get "taped," as we call it to make regulations, so I know not everyone is technically overweight or obese. Nevertheless, this is a big problem for young people. But I want to make sure that I am careful how I maneuver through these waters to make sure I don't say anything offensive. We currently live in times when body shaming someone can ruin you, and that is not what I am here to do. Plus, I don't want "cancel culture" and social media on my you-know-what. However, many of us are promoting obesity.

We all know or should know that this has associated health risks. Let's pause, though, so that I may make it very clear that I am no longer 140 pounds, and I have pants that do not fit. So, I don't want anyone to get the impression that I think "I have my thing on a string" if you remember that from earlier. I just want to make people aware, and that's all I've attempted to do thus far. Having extra body fat can lead to things like diabetes and hypertension. I would hate to burst your bubble, but yes, I have hypertension. I had it at 140 pounds, and I currently have it.

Although I think millennials are active in things such yoga, physical fitness, and healthy eating habits, we still are facing a growing issue. I know this may come as no surprise to older folks because all they think we do is eat avocados and play on our phones. But many millennials are dealing with weight and health issues. In fact, this can lead to missed time from work and less productivity.

In fact, Barkin, Heerman, Warren, and Rennhoff (2010) state, "As Millennials enter the workforce, the growing prevalence of obesity among their generation may negatively impact their productivity and resulting economic prosperity. Given that most of one's adult life is spent on the job, employers have a unique opportunity to contribute to the solution by creating an environmental culture of health." I know how hard it can be to deal with life and family all while trying to squeeze in some time to work-out. So, I am not judging, but since we are known as the entitled ones, then yes, companies should create a health-conscious culture, especially since we spend most of our time at work, are just as job-loyal as previous generations, and are the largest generation in the workforce. Somebody must keep the wheels turning, so it may as well be us little entitled bastards. I didn't mean any offense by the way; I'm just saying.

I can't speak for anyone else, but in my family and in a lot of black families, we hear the phrase "high blood pressure," also known as hypertension, quite a bit. My grandmother would constantly complain about her "pressure," as we tend to call it. My mom, the same, but who would've thought that just in my thirties, I would also be diagnosed with "pressure" or hypertension. This disease is known as the silent killer, and it is one of the top killers of black men.

This really comes as no surprise. What is surprising is that many more young people are battling with hypertension. There are lots of things that can raise blood pressure such as alcohol consumption; cigarettes; sodium; lack of exercise; and, of course, genetics. Blood pressure rises and lowers quite often. But it is when it continues to be high that you risk kidney issues and the worst of the worse, stroke and heart failure.

This is alarming that the rate of hypertension among young people is rising so drastically. Some of this may be due to stress, but I am surely not a doctor. So, don't quote me on that one. I mean having a ton of debt and maybe being slightly behind in life could really make your blood pressure go up. Just imagine trying to purchase a home and start a family all while carrying student debt and working a dead-end job. Sounds like hypertension in the making to me.

Now, some may say that I am just making excuses for young people or, you know the favorite, "Well, back in my day ..." But either way, just as much as people are concerned about obesity, they should also shed a little light on hypertension. These two things can go hand in hand, so a healthy diet and exercise could help with both of these conditions. But as I've said pretty much throughout the whole book, I am just here to bring awareness and hopefully understanding to the fact that millennials are fighting their own silent battles all while being hated on or often mistaken for those from Generation Z.

Things such as social factors can also play a part in developing hypertension. Blacks, Hispanics, and Latinos tend to be affected by social factors more than those from other races and ethnicities. Lack of healthcare and consuming processed and fast food plays a major part in this. Not to say that this isn't the case among others, it's just more prevalent among Blacks, Hispanics, and Latinos.

So, since I am only here to shed light and provide a source of information, let's look at a few statistics dealing with millennials and hypertension. Healthcare is extremely expensive especially in a country that is very technologically advanced. These costs will only continue to rise if young people continue to live unhealthy lifestyles. I always find it interesting that millennials are unhealthy in comparison to previous generations. Maybe because when it comes to mind, I think of people cleaning bullet wounds with liquor while the injured bites down on a piece of leather.

I know that this is a time before baby boomers and Gen Xers, but you must admit it is funny. Anyway, millennials are in a bind, and something must be done; and it must first start with young people becoming aware of their poor habits and correcting them. They always say if you want help, you have to first want to help yourself. Unfortunately, often having health issues causes other health issues, so having hypertension can lead to other problems. Just to show how this can become a domino effect, " According to the BCBS Health Index, people with hypertension are 2.7 times more likely to develop high cholesterol, 3.6 times more likely to be diagnosed with type 2 diabetes and 3.5 times more likely to be diagnosed with CAD than the general American population. They're also 5 times more likely to experience a stroke or heart failure" (Slachta, 2019).

Therefore, hypertension isn't something that you should ignore or take lightly. I know I sure do not. Hopefully most of us want to live as long as we can. I surely do, so I am focused on gaining control of my health. Hell, if can live to be seven hundred years old I will. But that's just me; some may not. Either way, take care of your health, young people, so you can focus on your vision and goals. It is said that if you don't make time for your health, one day your health will make the time for you, and by then, it may be too late.

Not to take anything away from the other generations. As I stated, I am sure they dealt with economic and health issues as well in their own way. But as you can see, young people are leaving this world way too soon to addiction and other health-related issues. And this has an impact on the world, an impact in the sense that many of them never get the chance to do what they were sent here to do, to leave a mark on the hearts of the people of the world. The cemetery is the richest place in the world because many people have taken to their graves businesses, books, and all sorts of things that could have been contributed to the world.

In the midst of dealing with things such as depression, obesity, increasing suicide rates, and hypertension, young people are still making a way, and please understand that although I have used the "young people" phrase quite often, when I write "young people," I am referring to millennials. This is not to take anything away from the Generation Z folks who are coming up, but this is just not for you. Millennials have their own stereotypes and labels to deal with. They don't need you guys getting any slack or credit for what they are doing. Just wait for you all's turn, and we millennials will see if we can come up with a few names to call you.

Hopefully, I haven't rubbed too many people the wrong way up to this point. I know some of my thoughts may be biased. But I love my generation, and I will not let anyone speak badly about us millennials, and I stand on that. I mean, I may have even pissed off a few millennials, but as my grandmother would say, "You'll be a'ight when the swelling goes down." My interpretation of that has always been that it hurts now, but the pain eventually goes away.

In fact, my grandparents and many of my elder family members had plenty of sayings, especially being from the south. I've heard things that made me feel confused. So, do not take it the wrong way, there is much knowledge, experience, and wisdom in previous generations. But please understand that young people have a lot the same. And one thing I cannot stand is a "do as I say, not as I do" type of person. It is said that "wisdom is obtained not through knowledge but through experience." And often I must remind people that being old or older doesn't make you wise. Being someone who comes from poverty and the "hood," and please excuse me for this in advance, I know quite a few experienced dummies.

Either way, young people are facing some crises, and if something isn't done to address this, it may trickle down into the generations that follow. Bad habits and beliefs are taught, and we must do something now so that health and mental issues are halted here.

CHAPTER 6

Rebels Without a Cause

MILLENNIALS

Hopefully, by now, most of you know that we are unique individuals and that we will never be the way that you all want us to be. It's just not the way life is. Also, hopefully, you older folks know by now that you all are just stuck in your ways, and in my personal opinion, a little bit salty or as they say nowadays "big mad" because you can't use a smartphone or understand emojis. I would also like to add that I hope most of you have an idea of the age range of millennials so that you can stop confusing us with Generation Z. We don't eat Tide Pods or sniff condoms. No shade, but if the shoe fits, then walk a mile in it. So, now that that is out of the way, we will continue to dig into the wonderful things that make millennials unique and just as good as any other generation.

As we know, millennials are currently the largest generation in the workforce and also the most educated generation. By the way, that may be why you old folks are mad and jealous because we're educated, but who knows? Anyway, no matter how you dissect it, we are working and educated. Again, doesn't sound like a bunch of lazy people to me, but I am literally no one; so my opinion is probably only worth the lint in your pocket. But I do know that it is worth taking the time to write this book so that everyone can back the you-know-what up off millennials!

Now a few will read this and say that I may be big mad myself, but guess what? I am because it is getting annoying that young people can't live their lives and seek fulfillment without being judged. But unlike all the other generations, millennials are quite different, and they believe in working together and having each other's back. The old saying "two heads are better than one" should be the motto for millennials, and here are a few reasons why. In a blog post, Saja Chodosh (2016) states:

> Millennials believe that successful teams strive for the perfect balance: a sense of openness to new ideas, people, and experiences, coupled by a recognition that everyone is an individual with different values, beliefs, experiences, and boundaries. Empathy and trust are key to finding this balance, as is a willingness to communicate freely within the workplace. Millennials look at building teams as ways to grow and widen perspectives and foster creativity and innovation. They see collaboration as key to any thriving business, and at a more personal level, it fosters individual happiness and social satisfaction.

There are quite a few things that could be learned from this statement, which I have mentioned to the point of exhaustion, such as the importance of being unique and being different. Millennials are hard to work and deal with because they aren't afraid to color outside of the lines, and this type of behavior makes people nervous. Another takeaway is that they are willing to freely communicate about their difference of opinions, ideas, and beliefs. Lastly, as I mentioned in the previous paragraph, the value of teamwork and collaboration and how people bounce ideas off each other leads to more creativity, insight, and innovation.

MILLENNIALS

If any of you out there come from having a military background such as myself, then you should know the value of teamwork and working together to solve problems. I do believe, though, that this is becoming a common thing among many organizations. You all can thank millennials for that. Okay maybe not, but I wouldn't be surprised if much of it comes from adapting to the millennials in the work force.

Look at sports, for instance. Lebron James is an amazing player, but it would be hard for him to beat five other guys by himself. Maybe he could give them a good run, but I am sure they would eventually figure him out. And yes, I am a Lebron James fan, so yes, he can beat five other players, not really, but yes, he can. As a matter of fact, millennials are the Lebron Jameses of the world, great players who will go down in history but are still hated on by everybody. That just seems to be the world in which we live; we never take the time to give people their roses while they are still here.

I look at teamwork as diversifying your investment much like with stock and real estate investing. If you have the risk of failure or lose spread across many people, then hopefully other members of the team will pick up the slack for those who aren't performing as well or who may be slightly behind in skill. Now, I know over the long run, this can cause problems. Trust me, I have been on a few teams that made me feel like I was doing all the work myself. But it gives those who may not be performing up to standard an opportunity to learn from others.

Let's make it very clear that times are changing, and young people just aren't into doing things the old way. This is not to say that anything is wrong with the old ways; it's just that sometimes things can be jazzed up a little. The traditional corporate structure just doesn't sit well with millennials, and I don't blame them. No one said you have to keep things the way they are to be successful, and sometimes fresh eyes and ideas bring fresh and possibly better ways of doing things. It truly seems to boil down to the fact that people don't like others who are not afraid to voice their opinions.

I find this to be an insecurity that exists a lot, especially with many Generation X-ers, people whom I have had the pleasure of meeting. Anytime you question the way something is done, they tend to get offended. You instantly come off as controversial or a know-it-all. Well, let me be the first to tell you that just because you say something doesn't make it right for one or the only way to reach the same results. This comes off as someone who really isn't confident in themselves. I've never had a problem being challenged or questioned because "a wise man knows that he knows not. Only a fool thinks that he knows all."

So, if you can't stand being questioned or hearing other opinions, then working with millennials may not work out too well for you. This has played a major role in changing corporate structure because millennials bring a new flame to the corporate world. As I mentioned, they love the idea of working in teams, but they also do not believe that you must have a title to be a leader. I can't say that I don't agree. We live in a world of titles and credentials, and everyone loves to give you their résumé, where they went to college, what neighborhood they live in, or what type of car they drive. Something I've noticed in my thirty-five years of life is that most of the time, it's the people without degrees or fancy vehicles who are making the big bucks.

Back when I started my janitorial company, I always struggled with this because I had degrees myself, and it bothered me the way people would sometimes treat custodial workers. That was until one day, I was cleaning a building alone, and someone was extremely rude to me. So, that night, I decide to research that person's job title and salary. Well, what do you know? My little six-figure-toilet-cleaning behind made more money than they did. Never did I ever allow titles and flashy things make me feel like I was doing worse than anyone else. Anyways, I said all of that to say that a title doesn't make you a leader, and it doesn't make you right.

Millennials understand this, so they focus on having challenging and opinionated work environments that allow everyone to have a voice. So, what if they want instant gratification and recognition. I mean, deep down inside, who doesn't, remember Maslow's hierarchy? Everyone wants to feel a sense of belonging and appreciation. Sorry, we aren't numb and inconsiderate of others like you older folk.

Previous generations come off as those who look to title holders such as supervisors or managers to make the big decisions. Millennials, on the other hand, aren't that way; they feel that anyone with the know-how and ability to perform the task should get it done. That strategy makes perfect sense, and I come from a military background where a twenty-something-year-old E3 or E4 has major responsibilities. In fact, when I was a twenty-one- or twenty-two-year-old E5 in the Navy, I had a prior enlisted O4 tell me, "Listen, you will never make E8 if you always have to ask for permission. Make an executive decision, and get the job done!" Those are words that will never leave my memory and words to which I think most millennials march.

In a nutshell, the average millennial doesn't care if you are the Chief Financial Officer, Shift Supervisor, or Front Desk Associate if you can get the job done. Having titles and credentials, at times, can go to one's head. As I said earlier, though, I do think people who put in the hard work and time it requires to obtain degrees and certifications should be rightfully employed and compensated. But having those things shouldn't make you feel like only you have the answers and know-how because if you take some time to research for yourself, you'll find that many successful people have no formal education beyond high school, or they went back to college after they became successful. There is still no school like the school of hard knocks.

Many say that if you find your passion, you will more than likely simultaneously find your purpose. And purposeful living is something for which I think we all are striving. Millennials are all about purpose; they are not fans of dead-end jobs and meaningless work. Up until this point, I've put forth about a sixty to seventy percent effort to not be too biased. Being a millennial and all, I to have to agree that waking up every day, going to do a job you dislike can be the most draining, demotivating, and depressing task on the planet.

MILLENNIALS

The fact that young people do not want to do any work that seems meaningless says a lot. Who in their right mind just does something simply because they have bills? And if so, for how long? I mean you gotta do what you gotta do, but that should be temporary. I believe it was Oprah who said, "Do what you have to do until you can do what you want to do." Nothing is more satisfying than waking up every day with purpose and passion. They say if you're doing something you love, you will never work a day in your life. The person who loves to surf and is a surf instructor is living the dream. This is the way young people think.

They only want to do things that mean something and to be acknowledged for doing a good job at it. I am a firm believer that sometimes you have to pat yourself on the back, especially when you are grinding toward making your dreams come true, but there is nothing wrong with a little "Congratulations" or "I am proud of you" along the way. That can really get the fire going when working on teams, supporting your children, or simply to let someone know to keep up the effort.

If that means being entitled or narcissistic, then hey, so be it. I grew up around toxic masculinity and men who have problems expressing themselves. And at times, I am guilty of it myself. So, I know the power of having someone say that they are proud of you. Besides, I have met plenty of sensitive and attention-seeking Gen Xers. So, let's stop making things that are basic human emotions and needs all about millennials. I cannot recall where I read it, but I saw once that "the way you see others is just a reflection of the way you see yourself."

Therefore, being able to spot the narcissistic behaviors of millennials just might mean that you are narcissistic yourself. Sort of like that old saying (Mogwai, n.d.), "I know you are, but what am I," which many kids used as a rebuttal "back in my day."

Many like to think of millennials as technology junkies which sounds a bit confusing to me. Because if technology continues to advance, simplify life, and improve the way we do things, then why would one continue to use old, outdated things? Would you rather listen to a baseball game on an old radio or be able to enjoy it on a nice 4K TV in your comfortable living room? I am sure I know the answer to that, and before any of the devil's advocates jump in, yes, I know watching the actual game at a ballpark with a hot dog and a beer, for those who are old enough to drink of course, trumps them both, but my point is that things improve and technology advances so that things become more convenient and enjoyable.

It's not our fault you baby boomers and Generation Xers have a hard time sending a text message or logging into Facebook. I had a hard time learning to use a rotary phone, but I learned; and I also learned to ignore that annoying pulsing sound my grandmother had on her phone when I was a kid. Again, yes, we millennials were around for those things, if I haven't made it clear enough already. No offense to my millennial peers; all millennials aren't created equal, but I still got love for you all.

Contrary to being tech junkies, I would have you know that there is one thing millennials should be bragging about, and that, my friends, is reading—yes, reading. Young people are out-reading previous generations. Now, I know some of that might be because many young people have had to read for the sake of obtaining a higher education, but regardless, there is a lot of reading going on. And if you all haven't heard it before, I would like to be the first to inform you that "readers are leaders." In fact, it is said that the average CEO or Chief Executive Officer reads in the ballpark of sixty books per year, which is roughly five books per month.

Reading is fundamental—at least that is what I was always told. I will admit I am a bit of a reader myself, and this is something I try to promote to any and everybody. It was once said by some old guy that reading books is "stupid." That person was just a hater and in his feelings because I am respected and followed by more people than he. That person will also be one of the first people bragging about this book or pretending he played a part in me writing it, yet he will remain nameless and unimportant. Anyway, as I come back to course, young people like to read, and we could name several benefits that come from reading; but I won't. I'll let you all go out and Google that information for yourselves.

In a recent article from 2019, Meagan Johnson states, "Millennials are reading more than older generations. They are more likely to have read a book over the past year compared to a Baby Boomer and Gen Xer and they read more than my generation (Generation X) did at the same age." Johnson also goes on to say, "According to Nielsen Books and Consumers, Millennial's physical book buying has continued to increase and now represents over 35% of the market. According to the same study, greater than 80% of Millennials are putting their reading funds towards books they can hold vs download."

So, let me get this straight: millennials are reading more than previous generations, and they are also purchasing physical books versus digital formats? Plus, we learned that readers are leaders, reading is fundamental, and the average CEO reads sixty books a year. Therefore, it would be safe for me to assume that millennials are well-founded, leaders, and future CEOs who aren't completely tech-babies since having the physical book is more appealing than the ebook, and for the old heads in the back that means electronic book.

Okay, I may have been reaching a bit by saying all of that, but good things always come from reading, especially if you are reading things to advance your career, to learn something to help start that new business, to improve your current business, or to just get ahead. This is not to say there is anything wrong with reading novels and fiction books, but I personally am just not a fan. Different strokes for different folks, you know.

Millennials are not big fans of traditional company structure and hierarchy. They believe in doing meaningful work that they are passionate about, and they tend to read more than previous generations. This is a perfect recipe and combination for future innovation. As technology changes and companies begin to change and adapt to future generations, these companies will need young leaders to replace those who will be aging and moving on from the working world. Millennials and Generation Z are on deck, and those young people will need someone to set the tone.

As you can see, many companies such as Google, Apple, and Amazon have built their entire corporate culture to accommodate millennials. For companies to continue to thrive, many of them will also have to make this shift. As frustrating as it may sound and as uncomfortable as it may be for most from previous generations, it is inevitable that as the boomers retire, the younger generations will take over the number of people in the workforce. In-house childcare, flexible work schedules, and team projects will soon become the culture of many companies to accommodate the younger crowd.

Millennials need their chance to show that they too are leaders and are capable of getting things done regardless of whether they are narcissistic and entitled. This is often a problem within many organizations where the older members and leaders aren't as open to the ideas of the younger crowd. It has been said by Marcus Buckingham (2016) in his book that "people leave managers, not companies." I agree, but I do think that if companies don't adopt ways to satisfy millennials, then many may also leave the companies due to it not being a good fit.

CHAPTER 7

The Internet and Beyond

MILLENNIALS

It's no secret by now that millennials are tech-babies. Many of them walk around with their heads buried in their smartphones and may be posted up at your local Starbucks on their laptops. The power of the internet has made the world a small place and has led to unfathomable innovation. People are becoming laptop entrepreneurs left and right, working on-the-go from their computers while traveling the world or sipping wine in their pajamas. Social sites such as Facebook and Instagram have their pros and cons, but I would like to think more pros than cons.

Social media has made the world a smaller place. In fact, I can honestly say that if it wasn't for social media, I would not have been able to keep up with old military buddies and people I met during my time in the Navy. I know it can become addictive for some because all they do is aimless scroll through hundreds or maybe even thousands of posts per day. I mean, I am guilty of it myself at times when I just want to spend some time closed off from things, but regardless of how annoying it can be or how distant it may make us all seem, you have the power to reach hundreds, thousands, and millions of people from your phone or laptop. This has created new industries and has made a lot of people very well off.

Just log on to Instagram, and you will see thousands of people claiming to be influencers and charging fees in exchange for posts in hopes of gaining followers and growing their social media accounts. In fact, if you own a business these days, having social media can play a major part in your business's growth. Things such as chatbots and autoresponders have also helped people and businesses run their operations twenty-four hours a day, giving them time to focus on other things such as employees and gaining new customers.

I am not a super fan of social media, and I don't have many followers, but I do understand the benefits that come with it if you use it for more than just wasting time and being in everybody's business. Since many of us spend so much time on our phones and social media anyway, we all should be looking for creative ways to use it to create a source of income. But we must keep in mind that Facebook and Instagram aren't the only forms of social media. There are platforms such as LinkedIn that many professionals use to further their careers and network with other professionals.

Social media plays a part in nearly everyone's daily routines with the exception of maybe baby boomers, but most of them struggle to operate a touch-screen cell phone. I probably didn't have to take a shot at them, but I did; and they'll get over it. There are quite a few social media platforms, and not all users are fans of them all. Some may like Facebook more than YouTube while others may choose Twitter, Instagram, or Reddit. In fact, a recent article by Cox (2019) states, "Social media habits are driven by people's individual interests, but their age can play a role in which channels they are drawn to."

It took me quite some time to get involved with Twitter, and it still is the least used social media account that I have. I just never really got hip to Twitter although I know it has its benefits, especially for business growth. For some, Twitter may be one of their most used accounts, but to each his own. I am sure I will become more into Twitter as things begin to transition for my business and life. YouTube is another big platform that has made many internet sensations along with Instagram.

No matter if you prefer Facebook over Instagram or Twitter over them both, they are a big part of most people's lives, especially young people. Nearly everyone walks around with a super-smart laptop, aka smartphone, in their pockets. So, it's kind of difficult to rid the world of it. The best thing to do is to just research and develop an understanding of social media and its impact on people from different age groups and to just accept that it may or may not be for you. Then live and let live.

Smartphones have helped make life and business simple and all in the palm of your hand. Now I personally am not here to debate which is better, the Android or iPhone. They are both great phones and come with their own unique features, and it all depends on the user. I have had Apple products, but I personally like the Android just as I prefer PC over Mac for specific reasons. The main reason is familiarity because I have used them for so long.

Regardless of which you may think is better, you have to admit there really isn't much that you cannot do from your phone. Not only can you just call and text from your phone, but you can send emails, schedule meetings and share calendars, Skype, Facetime, and electronically sign documents. To be completely honest, I cracked my laptop in 2014 and literally did everything from my phone for a few years before purchasing a new laptop, which still takes a back seat to my phone unless I just really, really want to sit upright and look at a bigger screen.

Speaking only from personal experience, I can say that many older people I meet are not into smartphones as much as millennials and Generation Z. Many of them just want to be able to send and receive calls. They are not big on text messages either. I have a friend who will respond to every text with a phone call so much so that I intentionally ignore their calls at times just because it's an inconvenience to me, and the text was the best method of communication at the time. I admit it isn't the most personal form of communication at times, but it has its advantages.

I recently had a doctor's appointment, and I was seated next to an older gentleman who received a phone call. As I looked over, I saw him pull out his nice smartphone and watched him peck away at the screen trying to answer his call. After about two or three times of his phone ringing, he was finally able to answer the call. That very small incident helped me realize how much things have changed and how different millennials are from baby boomers. The equivalent would be to ask a sixteen-year-old Gen Zer to work a twist-dial black-and-white TV with rabbit ears. In fact, many younger millennials probably wouldn't know how to work one either.

Someone once said that technology changes every seventy-two hours. Now, I don't know how true that may or may not be, but it is something to make you think. As we just mentioned, look at how social media and smartphones have changed the world from the way we do business, interact with family and friends, and even the rise of things such as chatbots. You may or may not know what chatbots are, but I am willing to bet that if you have done anything online, then you have some experience with them. Have you ever visited someone's website and a little box popped up asking to assist you? More than likely that was a chatbot, a computer program created to interact with and respond to people.

Now, again, I am no expert when it comes to technology, but I personally think chatbots are cool. According to *Chatbots Magazine* (Schlicht, 2016), "A chatbot is a service, powered by rules and some-times artificial intelligence, that you interact with via a chat interface. The service could be any number of things, ranging from functional to fun, and It could live in any major chat product (Facebook Messenger, Slack, Telegram, Text Messages, etc.)." As you can see, they can be used in many ways, and as I stated, we have all probably had some sort of involvement with them. You're probably also asking yourself what the hell that has to do with this book, but bear with me as I am about to attempt to drive it home.

Up to this point, I am sure it is no secret that people and, more importantly, millennials love convenience. I know I sure do, and I am an introvert; so talking on the phone and having a lot of human interaction isn't always on my list. And for those of you who are like me, chatbots are helpful when contacting customer service and things of that nature.

Based on some of my own personal experiences, it is very common for you elders to call as you prefer speaking to someone whereas the millennial crowds aren't big fans, and I say neither am I unless it is necessary as I know certain cases require making a call to get the job done. So, no need to feel awkward or out of place if you are not one for phone conservations because most millennials are not as well. In fact, in a blog titled "60% of millennials use chatbots. Are you empowering or alienating them?" (2019), it was stated that "Millennials prefer not to talk on the phone—as phone calls are perceived to be disruptive while text messages can be viewed at the recipient's leisure. Millennials prefer a casual and conversational communication style when it comes to interacting with businesses and chatbots fit the bill perfectly. Research shows messaging apps overtaking social networking in terms of adoption and usage."

As you can see, many, like myself, are big fans of being able to resolve an issue about an order with a chatbot rather than waiting on the phone for a representative. I am not sure if any younger millennials know anything about this, but I remember being a young kid going to our local video stores to rent movies and video games. Blockbuster was the big-shot store near our home. We only went to Blockbuster on payday. Anyway, I wrote all that to state that one thing millennials do differently from previous generations is the use of streaming services.

I was just a young whippersnapper when Netflix came around. In fact, back then—yes, I said back then like I am old—back then, Netflix would send you DVDs in the mail, and you were doing it big if you had a Blu-ray player. That was like having one terabyte of memory back then. In the blink of an eye, they had things like Hulu, Sling, and

MILLENNIALS

Amazon Prime streaming. Man, when I think about it, I am getting old myself. Soon I am going to be telling young kids how our music was so much better than theirs, and back in my day we didn't do things like this and that. Wow, that's funny to even think about, but hey, we all will have our time to be the old, disconnected, unhip person. In fact, since people like to judge millennials so much, allow me to share with you something that was said about Generation X years ago.

An article written by Williams (2019) about Gen X in the 90s states, "'They have few heroes, no anthems, no style to call their own,' wrote *Time Magazine* in a 1990 cover story called '20-something' that marked our debut, as a class, on the national stage. 'They crave entertainment, but their attention span is as short as one zap of a TV dial. They hate yuppies, hippies and druggies. They postpone marriage because they dread divorce. They sneer at Range Rovers, Rolexes and red suspenders.'" So, please have a nice large piece of humble pie. For some reason, I just felt the need to throw that in there since we millennials seem to always be under attack.

I am not too sure about that "zap" of a TV dial, especially in the 90s, but streaming, on the other hand, has led to the rise of the binge-watcher. I personally don't watch much of the latest series, so don't look to me for a conversation about *Money Heist* or *Tiger King* because I haven't seen a single episode. For the average millennial, though, this may not be the case. In fact, "60% regularly use subscription VOD solutions like Netflix, Amazon Instant Video, Hulu Plus and HBO GO. Other generations report utilizing free and subscription services 40% of the time" ("Millennials: The Streaming Generation," 2014). I will admit, though, I do prefer things such as Netflix over flipping through channels that cost an arm and a leg. And there's usually nothing worth watching on television anyway. Streaming is the future, and many providers may even begin to switch.

CHAPTER 8

Not Created Equal

MILLENNIALS

I will be the first to admit that I am all for millennials, you know, being a millennial myself. But I will also admit that I don't think that I am anything like someone who is twenty-five years old. Yes, someone who is twenty-five and someone soon to be thirty-five are both millennials, not some nineteen or twenty-year old for those of you who like to use the term "millennial" without knowing who millennials are. Anyway, I say that we are not all alike because we are at different stages in our lives, but I take nothing away from them because they are still my millennial brothers and sisters in arms. And no matter what, I am here to set the record straight for all of us.

A few friends and I have come up with our own terms to call those millennials who are thirty and older. We did this because although we are millennials, we tend to have some Generation X tendencies. Not that that's something important or that we care to be anything like them. Regardless, we tend to conduct ourselves slightly differently from those on the younger side of the millennial generation. I mean, let's just be honest; for those of you who are in your thirties and older, you all know what you were like at twenty-five. I don't think that has to do anything with generations but more so with just being young, lost, and living like a rock star.

In fact, if you are part of a generation prior to the millennial generation, then I am sure you can see a difference in your life at twenty-five and thirty-five. I am willing to bet that you had a few things going on that your parents and grandparents didn't really approve of or may not have aligned with their teachings. Just admit it; you don't like the fact that millennials have no problem admitting they want to be rewarded for working hard and accomplishing things while you all thought working hard until your back wasn't any good and money was money if it paid the bills was the way to go. Times change and people change, so just get over yourselves. Millennials are on deck, and when you are old and feeble, we will be doing things our way.

Hopefully, by now, you all are like, "Okay, get to the point. What's the term?" I had to build up some sort of suspense and keep you all reading. I wouldn't be doing a good job if you put the book down by now. Anyway, we like to call ourselves "elder millennial," a term that we use to separate the thirty-and-up millennials from the younger bunch. I am not saying that we don't share similar characteristics and thought processes. I am just simply saying we've had more time to figure out a few things and mature a bit.

I am not acting as if I don't have college debt, am unmarried, and don't own a home. A few of those are by choice, but we elder millennials have had time to work a few jobs, make some mistakes, and set clear career and life goals whereas someone who's in their twenties may just be grabbing life by the horns, and things may not be what they seem. I know at twenty-five, my life was pure hell, and I had made enough mistakes for myself and probably enough for another twenty-five-year-old. Either way, it was my life just like it's every other millennial's life, and I know without a shadow of doubt, we will all figure it out.

Let's stop acting like we all owned homes, had a family, and $750,000 stashed away for retirement at twenty-five. In fact, most people of previous generations probably didn't have all those things at forty-five. Life, like all things, takes time—time to figure out who you are, time to accumulate wealth, and time to be successful in our careers and businesses. Sorry, the average millennial didn't have it figured out at twenty-two fresh, out of a four-year degree. We must have missed the train, and yes, I meant everything I just wrote with the utmost sarcasm possible.

After a few moments of Google searches, I found that there is a micro-generation between Generation X and millennials. Born between 1977 and 1985, this group of people is known as Xennials or the Oregon Trail Generation, which would make those people between the ages of thirty-four and forty-three, slightly older than the typical age range designated for millennials. Again, in my humble opinion, these are a group of people trying to distinguish themselves from younger millennials. I personally don't think I or anyone else has anything against them. It's just that the term "millennials" has almost become profanity and is like calling someone out of their name.

The term was coined in 2014 by Sarah Stankorb in *Good Magazine*. This term is becoming common, and at some point in the near future may become some sort of subgroup for those who aren't quite millennial and also not quite Gen X. In fact, some have begun to evaluate what makes them different from those two generations. I will state I don't always feel like I am a millennial, but just out of pure spite for previous generations, I refuse to be Gen X; and of course, I am way too young to be a baby boomer. Also, by the way, the echo boomers are the only boomer generation I am rocking with.

Xennials are also called the Oregon Trail Generation because of a computer game that was popular when they were growing up. I am not too sure if many people remember this game, but I do; and it was one of the best games ever! I loved the days of elementary school when we would visit the school library, also known as the computer lab, because this would give me the opportunity to play *Oregon Trail*. I don't think I am old enough for the original version when you had to type words in a certain amount of time for a successful hunt, but I was around to fire the single shot gun with the little musket-ball-looking bullet. It was such an amazing game I would play it right now today as if it was just released on Xbox One or PlayStation 4. A few people probably don't know of this game, and if they do, it's some of the later versions of which I was not a fan.

There was also a time when many Xennials or elder millennials, as we like to call them, spent time online with dial-up services. The internet to us was America Online, aka AOL, and going back and forth in chat rooms. That was our version of Messenger and sliding into someone's DM. We had stereos and played cassette tapes. When we wanted to hear our favorite songs, we would have to wait until it was on the radio and record it onto our cassettes by placing pieces of paper in both corners. It was often a task getting the tape back on the roll after your stereo decided to eat the tape up. You were super fancy once you had a stereo with a CD player even though my mother rarely was willing to pay nearly twenty dollars for a CD.

Those were the days, which is why I say we are not all created equal because many younger millennials may not have heard of or even seen these things at some point in their lives. They didn't get a chance to experience them like those who are well into their thirties. The Xennials were the last group of people who truly played outside. We would spend all day outside playing things like basketball, kickball, and manhunt, which was our supercharged version of hide-and-seek. The only time we were allowed inside was to eat—we drank water from the hose out back. When my mother moved into public housing, the only rule was to be in by the time the streetlights came on.

Although one of the most stereotyped and criticized genera-tions around, most people are completely confused about millennials. It's just a term people throw around as some sort of insult for young people. Yet, millennials had the privilege of living between genera-ions. They are the last generation to see a lot of things that were on their way out such as floppy disks and manual car windows. The world technologically revolutionized right before their eyes. It was probably one of the best times to be young and carefree.

As it was stated earlier, elder millennials or Xennials do not feel that they are on the same page as younger millennials. This is mainly because they set the age ranges for generations at about fifteen years or so. It's no secret that I am not the only person who feels this way. There are plenty of older millennials who just don't want to be associated with the generation at all. Let's just face it; a lot can happen over the course of fifteen years. I would probably have a hard time dealing with someone who's thirty-seven years old who still acts the same way they did at twenty-three.

The term "millennial" has slowly moved away from being the name of a set group of individuals to a term that is offensive and somewhat degrading. In 2017, Singal states that "the dissociation I'm feeling from my own generation is partly an inevitable artifact of the artificial way we construct generations in the first place." It is almost like the divide-and-conquer tactic. Many have used "millennial" in such a negative way over the years that they have turned the generation against itself. This is a generational civil war, and there's no winner— just a group of people living life to the best of their abilities with the best with which they have to work.

Someone handed this generation a terrible economy and high price tags on everything. I'm not sure how many of you are familiar with the card game Spades, but if you are, then you will be able to understand this next statement. Being a millennial is like playing a game of Spades without any spades—not impossible, and you may even turn a few books—but it is going to be a very difficult game without any spades. Perhaps it's like playing Monopoly without being able to collect $200 whenever you pass go. Younger people are being bashed for who they are while older millennials are trying their best to not be part of it at all.

CHAPTER 9

Two Crises

MILLENNIALS

Earlier the Great Recession of 2008 was brought up a bit, and this had a major effect on Generation Y. This was one of the worst times many of us had seen since the Great Depression, and for some of us, ever, especially millennials who were all young adults just getting started at life. Many were still in college or just about done with college, and something that no one had ever thought to prepare for or ever thought would happen in their lives.

The housing market went belly up, and many banks had to be bailed out, in my opinion, because of unethical lending practices. Homes are a good way to create wealth, and many people had a large portion of their wealth tied into their homes. So, we all know how that played out and the effect that it had on the wealth gap. Well, for millennials, they didn't have any wealth or homes because they were just getting the ball rolling in life. The recession was so devastating that millennials became known as the "lost generation" in terms of wealth.

If you haven't noticed by now, there are many terms used to describe millennials, probably more than any other generation ever. They are known as the millennials, Generation Y, echo boomers, and the lost generation. This alone says a lot about this group of people as they have spent most, if not all, their lives under a microscope and under the scrutiny of the world. Being known as the lost generation is term specifically geared towards the economic state of the generation. Just imagine being a young adult facing a stiff job market and wage stagnation with no solution in sight.

I will state that the Great Recession had nothing to do with the personality traits of millennials, but it did help set them back and create a dark financial cloud over their heads. Some say that is the main reason many millennials are financially behind in life. This claim was also made in an article from *Business Insider*, in which Hoffower states that "according to a 2018 report by the Federal Reserve Bank of St. Louis. As of 2016, people born in this decade had wealth levels 34% below where they would most likely have been if the financial crisis hadn't occurred."

This led young people on a downward financial spiral and is one that will take many years to recover from. College debt was one of the most significant setbacks of the Great Recession, but we have spoken on that quite a bit; and there's no need to beat a dead horse. Nevertheless, this crisis devastated the average millennial, and they were never given any type of assistance or resources to recover. Older millennials took the hardest hit because they were already in the job market and competing while younger millennials came along when the economy was recovering. Did this play a part in millennials' entitled mentality? Who knows, but wouldn't you feel a little entitled if something was destroyed and you were left to deal with it?

Millennials have been building a house on an unsteady foundation since the Great Recession. And we must admit they did an okay job, but we weren't sure then and are not sure now if that building will withstand the test of economic times. Though this is normal with economies at times and because America has always done a good job at recovery and maintaining a thriving economy, we got over the recession and kept on with our lives. Then, out of nowhere, the unthinkable was on the brink of happening again, and this time, millennials were standing at the end of the barrel of a shotgun.

Nothing could have been more unfathomable than the COVID-19 pandemic. We have all heard of things such as Spanish flu and bubonic plague, but I don't think any of us were equipped or prepared to deal with a pandemic in our lifetimes. Imagine going on with your daily life and then a virus outbreaks and you think this won't be much different from Zika or Ebola. Then the next thing you know, China is shut down, America is restricting travel, and Italy has an alarming death toll. But I am not here to speak about the pandemic itself as I am aware that this has devastated many families and has led to quite a few unfortunate deaths.

I would like to turn your focus toward the effect that this pandemic has had on many nations and their economies. Millennials are, unfortunately, again in a financial crisis due to the effects that the pandemic has had on the American economy although America did come up with a $2.2 trillion stimulus plan to save the economy, and most American people received a $1200 stimulus check. It sounds good but not for a group of people who were still in economic recovery in the first place.

When will this group ever get a chance to establish some sort of wealth for themselves if they continue to get hit hard by tough economic times? They say the best way to get yourself out of a hole is to stop digging, but what do you do if you are not the one who's doing the digging? What do you do when someone has thrown you into a hole and has started piling dirt on top of you? Millennials are facing diminishing returns. According to Sean Illing (2020), "The Great Recession upended the economy as many millennials were entering the labor force for the first time. The pandemic and the resulting economic shock have hit as many are entering their 30s and could erase any gains they've made."

These are a resilient young bunch, to say the least, to have to deal with two economic crises all within a little over a decade. Yet, they are still working hard, pursuing education, and attempting to start families and live the American Dream. I can't think of a tougher group of people, so these people have earned the right seek a little instant gratification and perhaps even a little government assistance. Therefore, I am all for things like student loan forgiveness for those who qualify and whatever incentives and programs that are available for this young, struggling generation.

To have to live through all this and still feel like you are the generational punching bag is phenomenal. Give a millennial a pat on the back and few words of encouragement the next time you see one because they are kicking ass and taking names however slight it may be. As we continue to deal with this pandemic and economic crisis that we are facing at the time of this writing, only time will tell what the recovery will look like and where Gen Y will be standing when the smoke clears.

Please do not think that I am excluding anyone who isn't a millennial and what they might be facing during these tough times. This is just the millennials' time to have someone stand up for them and fight for their understanding. So, allow them to have their moment, and maybe we can give some praise to others on the next go around. This group has seen so much economic hardship, and the oldest of the generation still aren't forty. To deal with an economic crisis around the age of thirty then again right before you turn the big four 0 is like going through military boot camp twice and still not graduating once it is all over.

Therefore, this group will turn out to be one of the best generations to ever live because they have seen so many hard times that they will have the skills to navigate through finances like no other. The recession and the current economic crisis due to COVID-19 should teach not just millennials but all people how to prepare so that if this ever happens again, they can weather the storm. If we all haven't learned anything from either of these situations, we all should at least gain an understanding of the fact that there are other things that can affect an economy—not just housing and stock market crashes or banks and automobile makers needing bailouts. Countries should put plans in place to deal with potentially devastating viruses in the future.

Merriam-Webster defines a crisis (Crisis, n.d.) as "an emotionally significant event or radical change of status in a person's life." We all have, at some point in our lives, experienced some sort of emotional or radical change. A crisis can have a major effect on one's mental health and overall well-being. Many millennials, as we mentioned earlier, are struggling with depression and alcohol and drug use. Does what the recession did to the economy have some effect on that? I do not know, but I wouldn't be surprised if it did. I also wouldn't be surprised if the current economic crisis doesn't lead to an increase in those areas.

Bills, debt, and financial hardship can really break your spirits, and millennials may have an even tougher time coming back after this event. The wealth gap is continuously growing, and the middle class is slowly disappearing. This is a group that hasn't had the opportunity to set aside much cash in reserves, and if they had, they may have had to tap into those as of recently. So, the question is what plan will be put in place to get back on the right track? I am not a financial expert and will not pretend to be. I just hope that, at some point, someone acknowledges that the "lost generation" has really been taking some blows in silence.

I know parts of this writing may have come off as a cry for help, but it is not. It is just the raising of a flag in hope that someone will see it and investigate the reasons for the flag instead of labeling and stereotyping this group of people for whom most people still don't know the age range. It is always frustrating to hear someone bashing millennials only to find out that the person doing the bashing is a millennial themselves. They are surviving and making a way out of no way, and they are superstars in my eyes because the game plan that they had was destroyed by the recession. Then after ten years of building and making a comeback, they get hit again when they have their guards down. Millennials thought that education was the key, but that hasn't proven to be of much use and neither have skills and trades as businesses are shutting down.

Many decided to step out on their own in recent years and start businesses and side hustles, which is a great thing and an avenue to creating time and financial freedom in the long run. But the recent economic crisis due to the novel coronavirus outbreak has caused many businesses to lay off workers and permanently or temporarily shut down. Businesses have life cycles, and not all businesses can stand the test of time. No one was prepared for this or could have foreseen it or was able to predict it in a business plan.

Many people are out of work, and millennials are dealing with another recession of their own since many were just getting their heads above water. After dealing with the setbacks of the Great Recession of 2008, unemployment rates have risen through the roof and have set new records in American history. In an article from early April 2020, Stauffer says that "a record-breaking 6.6 million Americans filed for unemployment, and the numbers will likely get worse. According to rough estimates from the Federal Reserve Bank of St. Louis, job losses could hit 47 million — an unemployment rate of 32.1 percent — during the pandemic."

Not sure what anyone else thinks, but I would never have thought that a pandemic could lead to an economic crisis this bad. But, then again, I am not an economist, nor do I have much financial expertise to foresee these types of things. Most Americans are probably in the same boat when it comes to this expertise. When there are viruses and diseases, I would just think that the Center for Disease Control and Prevention would issue a few rules to get things under control, and back to normal we go.

I once heard a Brian Tracy seminar, and he said that every three to four months, a person usually experiences some sort of crisis, that life was a continuous cycle of "problem, problem, problem, crisis." If that is the case, then the average millennial experiences this, but once every decade or so, they experience a catastrophe. It becomes a cycle of two steps forward, one step back, and then they sprain their ankle and must sit out for a couple weeks.

This generation has been one of the most economically challenged generations all before developing a few gray hairs. They will have to be innovative and adaptable to come back from two economic hits, especially during a time when an expensive education is not worth its weight in the toilet paper the world is currently going crazy over. When the job market has taken a hit perhaps worse than the Great Recession hit, what does the future hold for millennials? Will they ever be able to create a financial foundation, or are they doomed to be the new working poor?

Only time will tell as industries and the global economy recover from the recent blow that millennials just took all within about a decade. Some say that economic hits can take decades to recover from. Millennials have been in a 12-round boxing match with Floyd Mayweather, taking a flurry of punches. Suddenly the bell rings, and the fight's over. Then, nope, here comes Manny Pacquiao fresh, all warmed-up, ready to beat them down all over again after just going 12 rounds with Mayweather. That may be a bit of an extreme exaggeration, but rarely does a generation take two economic hits in that short of a time period. Granted, no one can predict when things like viral outbreaks may happen and the effect that they may have on the economy due to shutdowns. But man, what a hell of a ride it has been for these young people.

Millennials are interested in making the world a better place, but this may prove to be a difficult task. For the generation that continuously struggles to get ahead economically, there is no reason to make excuses or play the blame game. But in the same breath, millennials are not to blame for the two economic hills they have had to climb. So what if they want instant gratification? So what if they may feel entitled? Does this have anything to do with the underlying economic issues that they have had to face? We get it; you all do not like the way millennials do things, and the feelings are mutual. Just like all other generations had their own issues, millennials have theirs.

All in all, millennials are a tough bunch, taking it all in stride and with a big smile on their faces. Can we all at least admit these guys have been hit by economic hardship, job scarcity, and massive debt like being hit with a tree trunk like in the old Bugs Bunny cartoons? Let's all think back to Maslow's Hierarchy and remember that all humans have basic needs that must be met in order to be motivated and productive. For baby boomers, it may have been different from the Greatest Genera-tion, and Generation X may have had different needs from baby boomers. Generation Z and Generation Alpha will all have their own set of characteristics and problems as well.

Is it also safe to say that we can come to an agreement that the term "millennial" has become somewhat of a fighting word to the point where many millennials who think they are not millennials attack other millennials, and to call one of them a millennial is like saying something bad about someone's mother or knocking a stick from their shoulder? A word that, at one point, meant a period of a thousand years became the name of a group of people, and then that word has become sort of an insult. One must admit that it can be annoying at times to constantly hear people bash on their generation, but you must remember that everyone and every generation has their own set of flaws.

Millennials do not go around making jokes about old people who cannot operate a smartphone or who don't know what "lmbo" means. Nor do they go around bashing people for not having social media accounts. This generation has lived through two of America's roughest economic times and has not complained about it once. You would think that they would be a bit more respected than what they are. They pursued education to the point that it became almost like an addiction just for the Great Recession to come along and shoot prices and the cost of living through the roof, leaving most, if not all of them, who chose to pursue education with an enormous amount of debt. Yet, still they fought through those tough times and began to rebuild their lives and be innovative in their living situations, their views on things like marriage, and corporate structure.

They began to save money and invest for the future only to wake up 12 years later to a global pandemic that indeed affected everyone, but also hit a group of people again who were still in the process of recovery from what happened to them in their early twenties. Again, there are no excuses being made for anyone because tough times do not last, but tough people do. When you look in the dictionary, the word "millennial" should be in parentheses next to "tough" because they have done nothing but tough it out all while being constantly criticized and made fun of. The name of their generation has been taken and tarnished and thrown around like an old rag doll.

This group is going to shock the world and make a comeback like no other. These young people have what it takes, and once they are in positions to implement change and restructure the way things are done on massive scale, they will really show the world who is the best. I will admit that I have somewhat of a personal feeling in all of this, but I am also understanding and open-minded. So, I will be the first to admit the flaws of millennials, but I will also be the first to highlight their strengths and accomplishments.

Somewhere along the way, things got crossed up, and millennials became the world's verbal punching bags simply for being different, for having their own ideologies, and for commanding change and understanding. If that leads to being considered entitled and narcissistic, so be it because no one ever said that there was a general mold to life to which every generation had to stick. At the end of the day, I challenge everyone to sit back and watch millennials work!

REFERENCES

60% of millennials use chatbots. Are you empowering or alienating them? (2019, November 25). First Source. Retrieved from https://www.firstsource.com/60-of-millennials-use-chatbots-are-you-empowering-or-alienating-them/?cn-reloaded=1

Barkin, S. L., Heerman, W. J., Warren, M. D., & Rennhoff, C. (2010). "Millennials and the World of Work: The Impact of Obesity on Health and Productivity." *Journal of Business and Psychology*, pp. 239-245.

Bialik, K., & Fry, R. (2019, February 14). *Millennial life: How young adulthood today compares with prior generations*. Pew Research Center: Social and Demographic Trends. Retrieved March 13, 2020, from https://www.pewsocialtrends.org/essay/millennial-life-how-young-adulthood-today-compares-with-prior-generations/

Buckingham, M. (2016). *First break all the rules: What the world's greatest managers do differently*. Gallup Press.

Chappelow, J. (2009, July 25). *The Great Recession* Investopedia. Retrieved March 8, 2020, from https://www.investopedia.com/terms/g/great-recession.asp

Chodosh, S. (2016, April 12). *Meaningful millennials: Collaboration and teamwork*. Emotive Brand. Retrieved from https://www.emotivebrand.com/meaningful-millennials-collaboration-teamwork/

Cox, D., & Thomson-DeVeaux, A. (2019, December 12). *Millennials are leaving religion and not coming back*. FiveThirtyEight. Retrieved from https://fivethirtyeight.com/features/millennials-are-leaving-religion-and-not-coming-back/

Cox, T. (2019, July 2). *How different generations use social media*. The Manifest. Retrieved from https://themanifest.com/social-media/how-different-generations-use-social-media

Crisis (n.d.). In *Merriam-Webster.com dictionary*. Retrieved from https://www.merriam-webster.com/dictionary/crisis

Curry, B. (2020 , January 17). *How to beat inflation*. Magnify Money. Retrieved from https://www.magnifymoney.com/blog/banking/how-to-beat-inflation/

Dickler, J. (2018, July 2). *How millennials are getting smarter about marriage*. CNBC. Retrieved from https://www.cnbc.com/2018/07/02/more-millennials-sign-prenups-before-marriage.html

Dill, K. (2020, February 19). *Millennials show loyalty to employers*. The Wall Street Journal. Retrieved March 13, 2020, from https://www.wsj.com/articles/millennials-show-loyalty-to-employers-11582118467

Eickmeyer, K. J. (2015). *Generation X and millennials: Attitudes toward marriage & divorce (FP-15-12)*. National Center for Family and Marriage Research Family Profiles. Retrieved from https://scholarworks.bgsu.edu/cgi/viewcontent.cgi?article=1076 &=&context=ncfmr_family_profiles&=&sei-redir=1&referer=https%253A%252F%252Fscholar.google.com%252Fscholar%253Fq%253Dmillennials%252Band%252Bdivorce%2526hl%253Den%2526as_sdt%253D0%2526as_vis%253

Ferro, S. (2019, June 26). *26 amazing facts about millennials*. Mental Floss. Retrieved from https://www.mentalfloss.com/article/586493/millennials-facts

Hoffower, H. (2019, May 24). *The US birthrate is the lowest it's been in 32 years, and it's partly because millennials can't afford having kids*. Business Insider. Retrieved from :https://www.businessinsider.com/us-birthrate-decline-millennials-delay-having-kids-2019-5

Hoffower, H. (n.d.). *The Great Recession created a domino effect of financial struggles for millennials — here are 5 ways it shaped the generation*. Business Insider. Retrieved from https://www.businessinsider.com/how-the-great-recession-affected-millennials-2019-8

Illing, S. (2020, April 21). *Millennials are getting screwed by the economy. Again.* Vox. Retrieved from https://www.vox.com/policy-and-politics/2020/4/21/21221273/coronavirus-millennials-great-recession-annie-lowrey

Johnson, M. (2019, January 28). "Millennials and reading – Do millennials read?" Meagan Johnson. Retrieved April 1, 2020, from https://meaganjohnson.com/millennials-and-reading/

Millennials: The streaming generation. (2014, February 2020). Broadband Technology Report. Retrieved from https://www.broadbandtechreport.com/docsis/headend-hub/article/16444476/millennials-the-streaming-generation

Mogwai. (n.d.). *I know you are but what am I?* Lyrics.com. Retrieved April 1, 2020, from https://www.lyrics.com/track/6349529/Mogwai/I+Know+You+Are+But+What+Am+I%3F

Parker-Pope, T. (2019, July 2). *Should we all take the slow road to love?* The New York Times. Retrieved from https://www.nytimes.com/2019/07/02/well/family/millennials-love-relationships-marriage-dating.html

Schlicht, M. (2016, April 20). *The complete beginner's guide to chatbots: Everything you need to know.* Chatbots Magazine. Retrieved from https://chatbotsmagazine.com/the-complete-beginner-s-guide-to-chatbots-8280b7b906ca

Shakur, T. (1993). Keep ya' head up. On *Strictly 4 My N.I.G.G.A.Z.* D. Daryl. Retrieved from Genius.

Singal, J. (2017, April 24). *Don't call me a millennial — I'm an old millennial.* The Cut. Retrieved from https://www.thecut.com/2017/04/two-types-of-millennials.html

Slachta, A. (2019, August 27). *Hypertension diagnoses rising fastest among millennials.* Cardiovascular Business: Strategies in Economics, Practice & Technology. Retrieved from https://www.cardiovascularbusiness.com/topics/hypertension/hypertension-diagnoses-rising-fastest-millennials

Stauffer, R. (2020, April 8). *Millennials were just starting to feel economically stable. Now we're being hit with another recession.* Vox. Retrieved from https://www.vox.com/first-person/2020/4/8/21211993/coronavirus-recession-millennials-covid-19

Thompson, D. (2019, June 13). *Report: Drug ODs, suicides soar among millennials.* WebMD. Retrieved from https://www.webmd.com/mental-health/addiction/news/20190613/report-drug-ods-suicides-soar-among-millennials#1

Tredgold, G. (2016, May 2). *29 surprising facts that explain why millennials see the world differently.* Inc. Retrieved from https://www.inc.com/gordon-tredgold/29-surprising-facts-about-millennials-and-what-motivates-them.html

West, K. (2007). Can't tell me nothing. On *Graduation*. D. Toomp.

Williams, A. (2019, May 14). *Actually, Gen X did sell out, invent all things millennial, and cause everything else that's great and awful.* The New York Times. Retrieved from https://www.nytimes.com/2019/05/14/style/gen-x-millenials.html

ABOUT THE AUTHOR

Delano Perry is a millennial, a certified life coach, and a Navy service-disabled veteran. He credits the Navy for shaping and developing his leadership skills that he translated into running his own successful janitorial business for years before finding his true passion in writing and impacting lives through coaching.

He suffers from post-traumatic stress disorder and depression, yet he has not allowed this to stop him from touching those who are fighting mental battles themselves. He provides powerful insight and guidance to other millennials who are struggling with mental illness. Delano refers to himself as the Hardheaded Millennial, spending most of his time around many people who are older than he.

He has learned that old methods do not always provide solutions for new issues, so he goes against the grain. He lives by the mantra "Frustration is just a sign of someone who wants to be successful." Delano brings passion and purpose, and although some days are rougher than others, he puts on that big smile and aims to inspire the lives of others on a daily basis.

The Millennial Speaker, LLC

www.themillennialspeaker.com

POST A REVIEW

Please leave your feedback on reading this book.

1. Visit www.amazon.com
2. Type in the search field the book's title, "Millennials," along with my last name, "Perry"
3. Scroll down, and click on "Write a customer review"

Let me know what you thought of the book and what you gained from it.

I read every review. They are tremendously helpful!

Thank you!